DROPPING MY LINES

DAN O'NEIL

Dropping My Lines
All Rights Reserved.
Copyright © 2018 Dan O'Neil
v2.0

The opinions expressed in this manuscript are solely the opinions of the author and do not represent the opinions or thoughts of the publisher. The author has represented and warranted full ownership and/or legal right to publish all the materials in this book.

This book may not be reproduced, transmitted, or stored in whole or in part by any means, including graphic, electronic, or mechanical without the express written consent of the publisher except in the case of brief quotations embodied in critical articles and reviews.

Outskirts Press, Inc.
http://www.outskirtspress.com

ISBN: 978-1-4787-9872-9

Cover Photo © 2018 Mandy Kivisto. All rights reserved - used with permission.

Outskirts Press and the "OP" logo are trademarks belonging to Outskirts Press, Inc.

PRINTED IN THE UNITED STATES OF AMERICA

Dad (The Fish Whisperer)

Table of Contents

Preface i
Prologue iii
Temper Temper, Dad 1
Super Duper 4
371 8
Let's Go Camping 15
Derby Days (Ouch!) 25
Oh, Danny Boy 29
Fiddler 32
Driving in Circles 42
My Goal 49
Eyeball 54
The Three Youngsters Go Fishing 57
M&Ms 63
Dream Fish 67
Beautiful Creatures 70
The Alaskan Woman 79
Ka-Sploosh 82
Coffee Anyone? 88
Halibut Don't Fight 92
Very Bottom 96
Hard Luck and the Silver Fox 98
Warning! 104
Bait! 108
Prankster 116
Stink Boat 119

The Meeting	123
Blame Game	127
Quick Study	130
Fog	134
Great Lifestyle	138
Plow Bait	142
Arley's Big Fish	147
Can't Stop Time	152
Big, Big Fish!	154
Until We Meet Again	163
First King Crab Season	167
Doubleheader	183
Hall of Famer	186
Good Day, Bad Day	192
Surprise	198
Mr. Fair-Weather	205
Great Scenery	211
Llama, Llama	219
Ralph	224
See You Next Year	233
Epilogue	236
Acknowledgements	238

Preface

DROPPING MY LINES is a collection of some of my favorite fishing stories from the past to the present. Over my many fishing years, I've compiled mostly memories of working as a saltwater, sportfishing guide, and with a few commercial fishing adventures mixed in.

I really had not planned on writing a book, but after recounting some of my memories with clients and friends, I decided to start writing down some of my favorites. At first, I would just scribble down a few notes from a memorable charter or commercial fishing trip to jog my fading memory. In the winters, while trolling for king salmon, I would look at my notes and begin putting my memories back together until I re-created my experiences. Writing a book while waiting for a big king to bite…what a great way to relax and put memories on paper.

Life is full of change, both good and bad. For me, one thing that has never changed is my love for fishing. Whether it's catching, fighting, losing, anticipating a bite, or just enjoying a stress-free, relaxing day on the water, it all adds up to one thing…I love to fish!

As you read through the short stories in my book, I hope to put a smile on your face as you meet my family, friends, and some of the characters with whom I've been so fortunate to fish.

A final note…some names have been changed (or forgotten) to protect the innocent. The stories, while not in chronological order, are true to the best of my memory.

Let's go fishing and have some fun…
Enjoy!

Prologue

Fishing

It is called fishing for a reason. If it was called catching, the mystery and adventure would already be decided dockside. There would be no great stories about the big one that got away. You know the one, "It was so big it wouldn't fit in the net." Or "It was a HOLY SHIT Fish. I don't know what it was, but it was the biggest fish I've ever had on a fishing line…and I mean ever."

I like to put the loser of the fish into two categories: the shouter and the pouter. The pouter likes to second guess why the fish is not in the boat. He or she will usually go inside the cabin and think out loud. *Was my drag too tight? Maybe a bad knot? I didn't leave too much slack in the line, or did I? Maybe the line had a bad spot? Did I horse the fish? Maybe I was impatient.* And the interrogation goes on and on to the point counseling may be needed. The shouter is very vocal when the fish goes on its merry way. Everyone and everything in a five-mile perimeter knows what this character is thinking. The explosion does not last long, just a few choice words and some fish name calling and it's over.

The excitement and satisfaction of catching a nice fish is truly a wonderful experience. When you get back from your trip, you can have your fish barbeques and show your friends pictures of your great catch and tell them the story of the big one that got away. You can make it as big as you want. The only picture you have is in your head, and it will be there for a long, long time.

In memory of

Sister... Dawn
A smile followed by an unmistakable laugh that brought smiles to all.

Mother... Pat
A loving mom. The ultimate poker bluffer of all time and I know firsthand.

Great friend/brother in law... Steve
We all love you; I see a big crab feed in the future.

Ted Sokol and Max Worhatch Sr.
Fishing buddies...Never forget the day Ted outfished us all. It was a miracle. I will always remember the drool coming off Max's mouth while he fought a king. He was eating it before he caught it!

Temper Temper, Dad

I AM FIFTY-SIX years young as I am writing this story. This is how I remember this particular O'Neil family king salmon fishing trip. Mom, Dad, Sister Dawn (who was twelve), Brother Dennis (eight), and I (nine) were headed out to Beacon Point on a beautiful afternoon in our twenty-two-foot Bell Boy boat. We skipped across the water heading to the hot spot about nine miles northwest of Petersburg. Mom, Dad, and us kids loved to fish. Family outings were always an adventure, and this fishing adventure was not going to disappoint!

We arrived at Beacon Point late in the afternoon. Dad slowed the boat to a slow trolling speed. It was the normal mad scramble to get rods in the water. Our lines were rigged with divers and leads, which were needed to get our double-hooked herring down to the various depths.

We trolled a couple of hours before my lucky mom hooked a king salmon. It was the typical Chinese fire drill—kids and Dad reeling our lines up so as not to tangle with Mom's fish. It's amazing how small a boat can get when you have five people and five rigged fishing poles with divers and leads flying around in the air tangling with brothers and sister. Dad was doing his best to gather rods from us kids and get them out of the way as Mom fought her fish.

Dad had the deck clean, kids out of the way, and the net was ready. Dad was good with the net. He was giving Mom instructions, "Pat, when he gets close, try to keep his head below the water and just guide him slowly up the side of the boat toward the net."

Mom fought the fish with perfection, run after run, and finally, the big king wore down. She slowly guided it up the side of the boat, and Dad masterfully swooped the net under the lunker. Dad had Mom's big king in the net and safely in the boat. It was huge, well over forty pounds…by far the biggest salmon Mom or Dad had ever caught.

The O'Neil family was ecstatic! Dad put the boat back in gear and began trolling. Some poles needed rebaiting. In the excitement, some of our baited herring had been stepped on and smashed. Finally, the gear was all reloaded and back in the water.

It wasn't long and Dad's rod went off. He had a king on and it was running like a big one. We got our rods out of his way and threw all our rods and gear in a neatly tangled clump off to one corner of the boat.

We kids stayed out of the way as Dad fought his big fish. We saw the fish once, and it was another lunker. It looked bigger than Mom's brute. It was a long thirty-minute battle, and the fish was finally tiring. It was time for the net. Mom had never netted a fish even close to this size, and Dad had never caught one this big. "Pat, this is what we're going to do. I'll bring him up the side of the boat, you put the net in front of his nose, and I'll guide him right into the net!" Excitement, tensions, adrenaline, and patience were at their peak. All was looking good.

Dad guided his trophy perfectly up the side of the boat. "Okay, Pat!" he said, as Mom put the net in front of his nose. That is when the shit hit the fan! Dad's fish went partway in the net and then turned out of the net. When Mom tried to get the net around the fish, the only thing she got was water and Dad's hooks in the net. Dad's quarry slowly swam away to live another day. The boat was silent.

Dad was standing there with a pole with no hooks, and poor Mom stood there with Dad's hooks in her very empty net. The first one to speak was Mom, "Kids, get in the cabin." We did, and she quickly followed.

She knew the look on Dad's face, and it was time to retreat to the cabin. His eyes were big, and he was uncontrollably shaking. It was the look we've all witnessed; the look when a small child falls on something hard. Eyes big, shaking, red face, mouth open, tries to cry, but no sound. Finally, they get a breath and then it comes…loud and long!

And then it came…loud and long. Dad was alone on deck throwing the biggest hissy fit we had ever witnessed. He was jumping and yelling while we all cowered in the cabin. Then he went on one more tantrum and there it went! He took the hook-less salmon rod and chucked it as far out in the water as he could throw it. I'm sure it was some sort of record for a pole toss.

"I quit!" Dad fired up the big engine and away to town we went. It was a long, quiet ride to town. Mom got the big one that day, and Dad got the big one that got away.

Super Duper

IN 1968, DAD purchased a commercial hand troll permit. His thought was to sell the salmon we were catching. Dad was a good sport fisherman, but commercial fishing for salmon was a whole new learning curve. He rigged our boat with big aluminum trolling poles and hand gurdies spooled with heavy wire. It would soon become clear that trolling with heavy line and big hooks made it a bigger challenge to trick a salmon into biting.

Dad would get all of his commercial gear in the water. Every fifteen feet or so he would have a snubber (piece of flexible rubber) connected to a flasher, and a leader off the flasher with a fresh herring or a rubber hoochie (imitation squid-like baits). There would be twelve to twenty different offerings in the water at the same time. Hour after hour, trip after trip of hand trolling…nothing, nothing, and more nothing. This hand trolling definitely was a new ball game, and Dad just kept striking out.

One morning Dad took the family out sport fishing. Of course, we were all excited because there would be no commercial trolling today, and chances were good we would catch something. We took the fishing vessel (F/V) *Little Dipper* just minutes away from town and began trolling for king salmon.

Dad, Mom, Dennis, Dawn, and I were all using leads and divers with leaders baited with fresh herring. You could never go wrong with fresh herring. Today, Dad was using a new spoon he had received in the mail. His boss had sent it to him, and it was billed as the newest gadget on the market and guaranteed to outfish anything. It was the newest and the greatest. The box said it swims like a wounded, screaming baitfish. How could you go wrong? The spoon was small and ivory colored. Dad put his new super duper in the water and watched it dance just below the surface. "Those fish don't have a chance. This should be outlawed," he said. We all laughed knowing if a fish was to be caught it would be on someone else's rod…the ones with fresh bait.

About half an hour had gone by and, to our great surprise, Dad's rod went down. He actually had a fish on! Dad was laughing and grinning, "I told you I've got a winner here!" Dad got the fish alongside the boat, and Mom got this one in the net. It was a nice twenty-pound king. Rods back in the water and *wham*…it was Dad's super duper again…this thing worked! Another twenty-pounder. Rods went back in the water and yes, super duper again…this time a sixty-pound halibut. Dad was ecstatic, "This thing catches everything!" The super duper caught every fish that day. Our fresh herring never even had a bite. It was Dad's day.

Dad could not stop thinking about his little ivory spoon that caught everything. Then the light bulb went on in his head—*What would happen if I put a super duper off every rubber snubber on the commercial gear? This is it*, he thought, *we're going to get rich, so rich*. He called his boss and got two cases of ivory spoons on the way.

The next weekend, Dad, Dennis, and I headed out to go commercial trolling. There was a hot bite at Snow Pass about thirty miles away. We left town at zero-dark-thirty in the morning. Dad had his new super dupers all tied up to flashers and to rubber snubbers. We arrived at Snow Pass mid-morning. The water was flat calm with balls of herring flying out of the water. It looked fishy, super fishy. There were five or six other boats already trolling in the area. Dad slowed the boat to a trolling speed.

It was finally time to start putting the gear in the water, the day of reckoning, time to become heroes or zeroes. The excitement, anticipation, the long wait was over. Finally, down went 1...2...3...4...5...6...7...8...9...10...super dupers on one side, followed by ten super dupers on the other side of the boat. All eyes were looking at the ends of the big aluminum poles, anticipating the moment when the big poles would start bouncing and the springs at the ends of the poles would start dancing. While trolling past a couple of other boats, we could see that they were catching fish. It was just a matter of time, and we would be too... just a matter of time.

Three hours later, the springs at the ends of the poles were still lifeless. After a couple more hours of watching other boats catch fish around us, Dad decided to pull up the gear to see if maybe it was tangled, or maybe the super dupers had junk on them. Something had to be wrong. It made absolutely no sense that we were not catching fish. The super duper catches everything. Dad started bringing up the gear, and the first spoon had a fish on it! A small fish, about the size of a herring...it was a herring! Second spoon had a herring. Third, fourth, fifth, the full load...twenty hooks out, and we had twenty herring. Yes, it was true. The super duper catches everything! We took all the herring off and again put the hot spoons back in the water, only to catch another load of herring. We had hit the mother lode, if only we were fishing for herring. The other boats soon saw what Dad was catching. The radio began to chatter. You could hear, "If anyone needs fresh herring, it looks like Bert might have some for sale." Poor Dad was not looking forward to making his next appearance at the coffee shop. Thank God he had a good job. Commercial fishing was not his gig. (Sorry, Dad, love you).

SUPER DUPER

371

AFTER GETTING OFF work at Alaska Airlines, my wife, Cheryl, and I decided to go trolling for a few hours. It was a beautiful May afternoon, and we couldn't get out on the water fast enough. Cheryl put together a quick bite and a couple of beverages for the outing. We dashed down to the dock and hopped into my seventeen-foot Reinell fiberglass boat. I started up her 140 inboard engine, untied the lines from the dock, and we were off. A short fifteen-minute cruise and we were in Scow Bay, where we would fish for king salmon. Scow Bay was close to town and a local favorite spot for early-run kings. I baited up our lines with fresh plug-cut herring, (herring with head cut off), lowered the tasty morsels about twenty feet down into the water, and began slowly trolling to make the baits roll. Cheryl found a sunny spot to read her book, and I tended the rods while we enjoyed the beautiful afternoon. We were not alone. There were nine or ten other boats fishing close by. We didn't care if we caught a fish. It was just a great way to relax at the end of a day, and if we did catch a king, it would be a bonus.

Cheryl and I trolling Scow Bay

After two hours of trolling with no action, I began trolling toward home. We were in no hurry to get back, so we decided to just fish our way to the dock. I was just trolling in the eddy of a navigational channel marker, and my rod took a slow, steady bend. My first thought was that I had snagged the marker. I yanked my rod and nothing budged. I tightened down my drag and pulled a bit harder, and I thought I felt something move but was sure it was just my imagination. Again, I put a little more pressure on my limber rod, and suddenly the line started peeling off my reel. I loosened up the drag as soon as I realized I had something huge on the end of my line—a real *holy shit fish*!

I yelled at Cheryl, "It's not the piling on that marker. It's a huge fish!" She pulled her pole out of the water and watched the show for a while, and then went back under her blanket and continued reading her book, knowing it was going to be awhile.

I had hooked the fish in thirty feet of water, right in the middle of a narrow channel. The fish would run almost to one shore and then turn around and come back at the boat and go to the other shore. The fish was fighting like a king salmon, but it felt way too big and solid to be a king. After an hour of battling, I had made zero headway on whatever was on the other end of my line. I was definitely not in control of this fish. It was completely in control of me. I was just trying not to break my twenty-five pound test leader.

The fish began running back out into Scow Bay, southbound toward deeper waters, and I just slowly followed with my small engine in gear. After two hours of chasing the fish around, I was now in the middle of Scow Bay in 120 feet of water. I was putting as much pressure on my line as I dared. Slowly I started gaining. Whatever I had on was coming to the surface to see what the hell was on the other end of the line. I hollered at Cheryl, "It's coming up to the surface!" She came next to the side of the boat. It surfaced just off the bow, and it looked like a huge moving shadow. When it swam alongside of the boat, I could see it was a monster halibut. It was damn near as big as the boat.

My new Oregonian wife had never seen a big fish, let alone something like this. Her eyes were huge, and she could barely muster out the words, "Dan, cut the God damn line!" That was not an option. We watched the giant effortlessly swim off the stern of the boat and slowly dive back toward the bottom of Scow Bay. I was sure that would be the last time we would ever see that fish again.

Other fellow fisherman had been watching and wondering, "What in the world is O'Neil doing?" A couple of buddies, Craig and Mickey, came alongside and jumped aboard to see if they could lend a hand. I had nothing on board to handle a big halibut. All we had on our boat was salmon gear, two wimpy salmon rods, and a net. Craig and Mickey rigged lines with big hooks on them, thinking maybe we could drive the hooks into the halibut's head, tie her off to a cleat on the boat, and tow it to shore. This fish was not coming aboard our little boat.

Craig drinking a pop while I'm playing fish

The halibut continued swimming south into deeper water. The deeper the water got, the deeper the fish could dive and the more line I would lose. It was all I could do to keep line on the reel. The tide started running, which made it hard to stay with the fish as we continued chasing it around. Then the halibut went on another long run. I couldn't believe it could still have this much strength after three hours of fighting. The halibut switched directions and ran almost all the way back to where I had originally hooked it. It ran straight down and just lay on the bottom. Again, I put as much pressure on the drag and rod as I dared. I'd come too far to break a line now. I tugged and pulled at different angles, but to no avail. We thought maybe the fish had tangled around a rock on the bottom and was gone, and I was left stuck on the bottom.

Just when I was ready to snap the line, I felt a small tug! Mrs. Big was still on my line. It had been four hours now since I hooked the monster, and it was getting dark. As I continued to battle the fish, the F/V *Howkan*, a large salmon tender, came alongside us and we were able to transfer onto the larger vessel.

The vessel was equipped with gaff hooks, hydraulics, a .22 pistol, and crew. I now felt like we had a fighting chance of landing this monster fish. I was gaining line slowly, but surely, and the giant was getting closer. Then, just like the first time, the halibut surfaced on its own and glided down the side of the boat.

I had relayed to Dan Vick, the skipper of the *Howkan*, that I thought the fish was over two hundred pounds. The skipper was ready with gaff hook in hand, but when he saw the giant, his eyes got huge. He quickly realized he was no match for the big fish. He raised his gaff up and we all watched the halibut cruise by. "Boys, get me the gun! This is the biggest god damn fish I've ever seen!" The halibut dove again.

Ten minutes later, she was coming up once more. The halibut surfaced twenty-five feet off the side of the boat and was swimming directly toward the boat. When the monster was about fifteen feet away, the skipper started letting the lead fly. Somehow, he missed my line and some of the lead hit the target. The halibut began to slowly sink.

We were just able to reach down and sink gaff hooks into the head of the halibut before it sank out of reach. The guys were unable to lift the halibut aboard due to the weight of the fish and the high sides of the *Howkan*. The next plan was to attach a line to a gaff that was already in the fish and boom the fish aboard using the boat's hydraulics.

The halibut was halfway up to the rail when the gaff hook began to straighten out! The skipper lowered the fish back down into the water. This time, a shark hook was stuck in the head and then tied off to the rail of the *Howkan*. Mickey and Tom Drennen then managed to get a line through the halibut's gills and mouth. The boom was then attached directly to the line, and the lunker was hoisted aboard.

I could not believe I had just landed the monster on a salmon rod and reel with a thirty-pound main line and a twenty-five-pound test leader. The *Howkan* dropped me off on my boat that was now adrift with Cheryl still on it! In all the commotion, we had forgotten to tie our boat off on the side of the *Howkan*.

The next morning the fish was weighed. The beast was 371 pounds and 92 inches long. It was the largest halibut of 1983 recorded.

DROPPING MY LINES

Unfortunately, it could not go in the *Guinness Book of World Records* for largest halibut for line class. To qualify for the book, a fish may not be shot.

Though I didn't go down in the record book, I did receive lots of Maxima line, hats, and leaders. I also got an article and picture featured in *Outdoor Life* and *Alaska Magazine*. It was a wonderful experience for a twenty-four-year-old man. If it happened today, I would cut the line.

Me and my big halibut the next morning

Let's Go Camping

ONE OF MY wife's favorite things to do is to go camping. One weekend many moons ago, Cheryl and I took the boat out and headed for our favorite camping spot, Thomas Bay. We would spend two nights in a US Forest Service cabin that we had rented. Though we were only going to spend two nights, we had enough food and gear for two weeks. I guess it's better to be overprepared than underprepared.

It was a beautiful July day with temperatures in the low seventies...a true Petersburg scorcher. After a cool morning one-hour boat ride, we arrived at our cozy little cabin. The cabin was tucked back in a scenic cove with huge spruce trees surrounding it. Just off one side of the cabin, a beautiful waterfall could be seen and heard gushing into the bay. Steep, snow-covered mountains surrounded the entire bay. There's no wonder we love coming to Thomas Bay. It has it all: glaciers, steep jagged rock formations, waterfalls, and an abundance of wildlife, including whales, seals, sea lions, goats, deer, moose, otter, bear, and, of course, the occasional Kushtikaw (which I still haven't seen!). Legend says people have claimed to see these devil creatures around 1900. They are described as looking like half man, half monkey-looking creatures with oozing, open sores and long, sharp claws! Thomas Bay is a nesting and feeding area for birds, including loons, eagles, ducks, geese, and a huge population of marbled murrelets.

As we arrived at Thomas Bay, I pulled the boat in as close to the cabin as possible. We began unloading the boat with all the camping gear we could possibly need for the next two days. We would not be roughing it! We had air mattresses, blankets, sleeping bags, more blankets, lanterns, a stereo, food for an army, and much more. If we got weathered in, we were set. After unpacking, we spent our first day beachcombing and playing cards. Late that afternoon while sitting on the deck, Cheryl and I witnessed Canadian honkers nesting in the nearby spruce trees. Yes, I said honkers in trees! We were sitting on the deck, nursing our glasses of wine. We could hear geese honking and carrying on. The honking got louder, and soon two honkers came flying directly at our cabin. They continued to fly directly at us, and then made a hard bank and circled back out away from the trees and cabin. This show proceeded for the next forty-five minutes (or two glasses of wine or so). Then it happened. We could hear the geese honking as they again made an approach toward the cabin. Soon, we could see them coming. They were much lower this time. I thought they were just going to land in the water in front of the deck, but they kept coming and then made a hard right turn off the deck. There was no way they were going to clear the trees, and they didn't. They both crashed into a big spruce tree. The two of us just looked at each other and at our empty glasses, and then looked with amazement at those two big-ass geese sitting in a spruce tree. We soon realized that they had a nest in the tree. While I knew that geese nested on shores, I was surprised to learn that they also nested in trees. I swear to God they landed in a tree! Hey, I had a drunk witness to verify the event.

LET'S GO CAMPING

Our home away from home for the weekend.

Here's the proof, goose in a tree

I never get tired of the scenery and the wildlife, but more than anything, I love to troll for big king salmon in Thomas Bay. I love fishing for king salmon anywhere, but there's nothing better than fishing in a place where you are surrounded by absolute breathtaking beauty. Often, we were fishing without another boat in sight, and sometimes even pulling up a beautiful, bright silver king salmon out of the turquoise-colored glacier water that fills the bay.

I'm still looking for my sixty-pound king, and my bet is that it will come out of this bay...maybe today, as I am trolling by myself and writing these pages. Nothing beats getting interrupted by the sound of a line tearing off the reel with a big salmon on the other end. If I get a sixty-pounder before I finish this book, it will have its own chapter for sure.

On day two of our camping trip, we woke up to a beautiful morning. It was a nice laid-back morning. Coffee, breakfast, and some cards, and then it was time to go rock hunting. Yes, I said rock hunting. My favorite thing to do (not!). Cheryl loves to stroll along the beaches and gather buckets of small sea-polished rocks and great big monster-sized flat rocks for her rock garden at home. Rock hunting has always been part of our camping trips (painful part). Getting the rocks in the buckets and putting the flat rocks in a pile is not bad. Getting the buckets and piles of heavy flat rocks onto the boat is a real backbreaking workout though. The fun doesn't stop there. Once we get our treasures back to town, we have to get the rocks from the boat, onto the dock, up the dock, into the truck, and finally from the truck to their new resting place.

All that fun, backbreaking work, and all the hundreds of pounds of rocks we have gathered, and yet our treasures barely cover a small area of the garden. It was going to take many camping trips and backaches to finish Cheryl's rock garden. They do sell rocks by the truckload, but Cheryl says, "It's just not the same!" I have to agree with her. If we got a dump truck load of rocks delivered, we certainly would not have the pleasure of so many backaches. It just wouldn't be the same.

After our day of hauling rocks to the boat, we retreated to our cozy little cabin. There's nothing like just relaxing with no phones, no TV, and no work to worry about. As long as the boat doesn't drag anchor, and we don't run out of beverages, we don't have a worry in the world. We spent the afternoon just eating, napping, and reading. The evening was spent playing backgammon, cards, a little drinking, and of course, more eating, before we called it a night and went to bed.

The next morning, I got up at 4:30 a.m. I quietly got dressed and snuck out of the cabin without waking Cheryl. Within twenty minutes, I was on the boat and trolling for king salmon. It was a beautiful morning, not a cloud in the sky. The best time to catch a big king is first thing in the morning, and I wasn't going to sleep in and miss a chance.

After only thirty minutes of trolling, my rod took an instant bend, and my reel came to life. Line began disappearing off the reel, and the tip of my rod was bending all the way into the water. I had a beautiful Thomas Bay king salmon on. After about a twenty-minute fight, the beautiful salmon was in the net—a nice thirty-five-pound king. Calm waters, and not another boat in sight, the most beautiful place in the world, all alone without a care in the world, fishing, and catching a big king…this truly must be heaven.

DROPPING MY LINES

goat watching as I troll along cliffs

Another twenty minutes of trolling, and again the rod tip dipped in the water. This time a nice twenty-pound king. I quickly cleaned my fish and put them on ice in the cooler, and back to the cabin I went. I anchored the boat out and very quietly entered the cabin. It wasn't even 7:00 a.m., and Cheryl was still sleeping soundly.

I made some coffee and stoked the fire. Cheryl was up and drinking her first cup of coffee and Caroline's by 8:30 a.m. We both drank our coffee and played some more cards. After a big breakfast, it was time to begin another glorious day of hunting for rocks (yea!). I had already fulfilled my day, and now it was time to help Cheryl enjoy the day…another beautiful day.

We gathered rocks into the later part of the afternoon. We were both beat from packing bucket after bucket of rocks from their resting place to the boat. After loading up the last bucket of rocks, I sweet-talked Cheryl into a little bit of king salmon fishing.

Cheryl is not real big on fishing, unless it's calm and warm. And it was. It's not about catching with Cheryl; it's about having the boat positioned so she is in the sun. We trolled for an hour with no luck. Finally, the moment I had been waiting for…Cheryl opened up the cooler to get a cold drink.

"What! Where did these fish come from?" She had no idea I'd gotten up early and gone fishing. The look of surprise on her face was priceless. I fished and Cheryl sunbathed for another hour, and then we retreated to our cabin. The rest of the day was spent playing games, eating, napping, and more relaxing.

Author with hair holding a beautiful Thomas Bay king…

The next morning, we both slept in. It was another clear and warm day. After coffee and a big breakfast, we began packing up for the trip home. It didn't take long. The boat was loaded up, and we were ready to say goodbye to our home away from home. It was just too nice to go home quite yet.

We decided to sit on the beach and have a cold pop in the sun before heading for home. Cheryl found a nice spot in the sand, and I rigged an anchor for the boat.

I put the anchor on the bow with about twenty feet of rope attached to the boat. I took another, longer shot of line and tied it off on the anchor. I pushed the boat about forty feet or so off the beach and then yanked on the second line I had tied to the anchor. The anchor pulled off the bow and splashed into the water, just as I had planned. I walked the line up the beach and wrapped it around a rock. The boat was anchored, and I headed up to join my beautiful wife in the sun.

We sat and drank our cold pops and soaked up the rays. Before we knew it, an hour had gone by. When I looked out at the boat something seemed wrong, very wrong. The boat was slowly drifting further away from shore. The tide had come in, and the anchor was no longer on the bottom. The line from the boat to the beach was also gone. Dan's Anchor Job 101 failed miserably. Our ride back home was slowly leaving without us.

Our wonderful camping trip had just taken a terrible turn. There was only one thing to do…strip down to my undies and swim to the boat. It wasn't that far away, and it was close to seventy degrees out. I was not much of a swimmer, but a fair dog paddler. Hell, I was only in my early twenties back then. I could surely do this.

There was no time to contemplate my decision. The boat was slowly drifting farther away. The time was now. I quickly stripped down to my shorts, ran down to the water's edge, and plunged into the glacial waters of Thomas Bay. Holy, holy, holy shit, it was colder than anticipated. I was sure my man berries had just dropped off. My wiener instantly went from an outie to an innie. There was definitely no extra drag going through the water; Thomas Bay had stolen my manhood! Despite being cold, it seemed like I was splashing through the water at a decent speed and cutting the distance between the boat and myself.

Five minutes later, I had cut the distance to the boat in half. I had begun to tire, and oh, my God, I was getting cold. My butt was numb and my cheeks were clenched so tight you couldn't fit a piece of notebook paper between them. I was frozen! I was over halfway to the boat, when I got a big surprise. When I went to take a stroke, my entire body uncontrollably went to half speed. Fear shot through me. Hypothermia was setting in. I stopped and treaded water for a few seconds, "Cheryl," I yelled, "I don't know if I can make it!"

The response from the love of my life was, "Well, don't turn back now, you're over halfway there!"

Evidently, she didn't do very well in math… I was over halfway, but the boat was drifting at almost the same speed I was dog paddling. I didn't have time to explain to my beloved the circumstance I was in, so I did what every smart husband would do; I began dog paddling for the boat!

I'm sure I looked like a wounded turtle going through the water. I was committed now, and I was either going to make the boat or I was going to drown in Thomas Bay.

Somehow, and I'm not sure how, I made it to the boat. I was so cold and exhausted, it was all I could do to pull myself over the stern and into the boat. I just lay in the boat for a few minutes. Life was great. I got my worthless anchor aboard, started the engine, and steered my boat back to shore and got Cheryl.

I'm a lucky man to be alive today. No doubt, if I had to do it over again, I would have just let the boat drift away and waited for help. You will probably get your boat back, but you only have one life. It's true: the older you get, the smarter you get. Life is too short as it is.

Cheryl had no idea how serious the situation was. Being from Portland, Oregon, and never being around boats and currents, she had no way of knowing what danger I was in. I had escaped the end that time and lived to experience many more wonderful camping trips with Cheryl, and later, our kids too.

Derby Days (Ouch!)

GOOD STORIES OFTEN come from bad outcomes…sometimes things don't go quite as planned. For a lot of siblings, working on a boat together does not work. My brother, Dennis, and I were born to fish, and we have always been able to work well together. Dennis had a dream to own his own boat and be a commercial fisherman, and I was set on being a fishing guide. We both succeeded in our goals.

Early in Dennis's commercial endeavors, I would go out on commercial halibut trips with him. Back then, anyone could get a license to fish halibut, and there was no set amount of licenses issued. The halibut seasons were very short. They could be as short as a day, or as long as a week. There was not a quota or specific amount of halibut you could catch. Each fisherman's goal was to catch as many legal (over thirty-two inch) halibut in that period as possible.

In April of 1982, my brother and I headed out on the thirty-six foot F/V *Sweet "P"* for a halibut opening. The season opened at twelve noon. We set all of our halibut gear and began retrieving our gear six hours later. We were lucky; we had set our hooks on some fish. The hooks were steadily coming back with nice halibut on them. The fishing was so good, we had to off-load our catch to a tender to make room for more fish. We were young and hard workers. We fished nonstop for about two days and nights and were soon going to realize that sometimes plans don't always go as planned.

It was around four o'clock in the morning, and I was taking a quick nap while Dennis finished hauling a set. I'd just lay down and barely had my eyes shut, when I felt a nudge. I opened my eyes to a horrific sight. The first thing I noticed was a big hunk of octopus hanging off my brother's hand. Then I realized that it was one of our baited hooks! The big halibut hook was embedded in his hand, with a hunk of the octopus we were using for bait still attached.

Dennis had been trying to get a very large skate (fish that looks like stingray) off a hook. He had reached down with a knife to make a cut in the fish's mouth so he could shake it off the hook. When he made the cut alongside the hook, the hundred-pound skate fell off the hook, and the hook snapped back, right into the base of Dennis's thumb. Dennis wasn't in a lot of pain at the time. He was just pissed. This was going to cost us time and money!

We cut his glove and the octopus off the hook so we could see just how bad it was. The big hook was buried deep into the meaty base of his thumb, barb and all. There was no metal coming out the other side, so we couldn't bring the barb through and cut it off to slip it back through. It was just ugly, and his hand was growing larger by the minute.

Dennis wanted that hook out in the worst way. After weighing our options, Dennis decided he was just going to give it a big yank and hope like hell it would come out. His thumb and hand were pretty much numb, so he figured it was as good a time as ever to give a good hard and quick pull. I was not volunteering for the job. We poured whiskey in and around the wound and then poured some more in and around Dennis's mouth. It was like a John Wayne movie.

Dennis grabbed hold of what was left of the shank of the hook and gave it a good, quick, healthy yank! Son of a bitch—that brought him to his knees. Holy crap, Brother Dennis's hand was not numb anymore! He was now in unbelievable pain, and the hook remained in its original position. He had just yanked against a bunch of entangled tendons, nerves, and muscle. Doctor Dennis and Nurse Dan were not going to get that hook out. More whiskey for the wound, and more whiskey for the skipper was necessary.

We went to plan B. Alaska Island Air dispatched a plane to come and get Dennis and get him to a more qualified doctor. Soon the floatplane arrived for Dennis. "Okay, Dan, you finish dressing (cleaning) and icing all the halibut on deck and then get some sleep, and I'll be back as soon as I can."

The plane flew away, and I began taking care of the halibut. The deck was layered with uncleaned fish. I began dressing and icing fish. About five hours later, as I was just finishing the last halibut, I heard the floatplane landing. Dennis was back! He hopped on the boat. The hook had been removed, and his hand was neatly bandaged. He was in great spirits. "Let's go haul some gear, brother! How was your nap?" He chuckled with a big smile.

We'd been going on nearly two days and nights without sleep and hardly any food. Dennis had brought back a real treat from town…a nice big deer roast. He put it in a roasting bag with veggies and spices and put it in the oven at a low heat. We were going to have a well-deserved meal tonight.

We continued hauling and setting more hooks. The fishing continued to be very good, and Dennis was managing with his big, bandaged hand. We had his bandages and stiches covered in a plastic bag to keep them dry the best we could.

Later that evening, the smell of the roast was too much, and we finally took a break for *real* food and a quick nap. The roast tasted great. We took a two-hour nap and both woke up sicker than dogs. The roast had tasted great, but it was spoiled, and we both had food poisoning. Yes, it was coming out both ends. Dennis had good intentions but talk about backfiring. And I mean literally backfiring!

After a day and a half of this, we had no more to give. We'd managed to continue working through these fun times on the toilet and over the side. This was not the extreme weight-loss diet we were planning on. We looked like a couple of starving Ethiopians. I'd dropped over twenty pounds off my already lean body. Dennis was looking pretty lean too. It turned out to be a very profitable season for two young brothers, but not without a little excitement along the way.

Large skate

Unloading halibut

Oh, Danny Boy

I'D MADE TWO mistakes on that July day. The first was returning home from my charter two hours late. The second, and biggest, mistake was not calling Cheryl to let her know all was fine and I was just running a little late.

It all started as just a normal routine charter. I had received a phone call from a gal who had a party of four that wanted to go see the LeConte Glacier and do a little fishing. Basically, she just wanted to spend a beautiful July day out on the water with her friends.

I got the boat ready and was awaiting their arrival. I was expecting two couples, but to my surprise, down the dock headed right for the *Julie Kay* were four not-hard-to-look-at women. They would be my charter for the day. They were on a girls' Alaskan adventure. Traveling in a small camper trailer, the girls were taking in Alaskan sights. Today, I would show them some sights and some fishing around the Petersburg area. Hey, it was my job and the bills had to get paid!

The girls had picked a beautiful day for the trip—blue skies, temperatures expected to hit eighty degrees, and light winds. We began the morning trolling for coho salmon. It didn't take long, and the girls sprang into action—jerking, reeling, screaming, giggling, and a little jiggling, but I paid no attention. The coho action was hot, double hookups, and even three fish on at once. They were losing more fish than they were catching, but it didn't matter because they only wanted a couple to eat.

After a couple hours of salmon fishing, the salmon rods were put away, and we headed up toward the LeConte Glacier. I was able to get all the way to the face of the glacier. My clients were amazed at the color and unbelievable sizes of the icebergs. I plucked a small iceberg from the water. It looked small when I went to grab it but was all I could do to lift it aboard. I chipped pieces off the small berg and offered the gals a beverage over the ice. They had brought their own beverages, and were soon having wine and beer over iceberg ice for their first time.

By mid-afternoon, it was back to fishing. This time, I anchored the boat and we tried our luck at bottom fishing. My clients were having a day to remember, and so was I. The temperature had risen to eighty degrees—a real scorcher for Petersburg standards. The girls caught a few cod and a few halibut. It took two women on one rod to wrestle up a fifty-pound halibut. They had barely any space in their camper for fish, so I let the fish go.

I surprised them and started the barbeque and cooked one of their salmon for a late lunch. It was a real treat for them, and it couldn't get much fresher. It went well with another bottle of wine. Before I knew it, I had four drunk hippie chicks on my boat. They had definitely loosened up. My name had gone from Dan, to Captain Dan, to Dan the Man, to Oh Danny Boy.

The Porta Potty was getting a lot of use by three of them, but the blonde gal preferred hanging her koochi pop over the side of the boat and letting hers fly. I just looked at the shoreline—what else could I do! It was hippie chicks gone wild!

After a great meal, it was time to reel in the rods and get back to town. I had been working so hard, the day had totally gotten away from me. The time was five thirty, and I was running late. By the time I docked the boat, it was six thirty. Cheryl would be worried because I had not called to tell her I was running behind schedule…big mistake!

The girls headed up the dock, giggling and staggering. They all wanted a Secret Cove Charters hat. I told them I had some in my truck and I would be right up to get them one as soon as I cleaned their salmon. I quickly cleaned the fish and put it in a bag.

When I got to the top of the ramp, my day took a huge downward spiral. There was my truck with my beautiful, not-so-chipper

OH, DANNY BOY

wife waiting for me in the driver's seat, and there were my four hippie chicks heading right at the truck. Short shorts, tank tops, and no over-the-shoulder boulder holders on (bra). Holy shit! I got there just in time to hear one of the brunettes ask Cheryl if she had any Secret Cove Charter hats. Cheryl replied, "Yes, hats are twenty dollars each." Then the blonde gal squeezed her head into the open window, and I heard, "Well, Danny Boy said his hats are free for us!"

Oh, Danny Boy was soon going to be spending some quality couch time. I gave out hats, sent the girls on their merry way, and went home with my not-so-merry wife. A strong, cold northerly had entered the O'Neil house, and it looked like the cold front was going to stick around for a few days! I tried to explain what a hard day at the office I had, and how I was so busy that the time had just gotten away from me. I was just digging myself a deeper hole. The more I talked, the deeper in I got. My goose was cooked. I was in for a long dose of the dreaded silent treatment. Oh Danny Boy set up camp on the couch to ride out the storm. For the record, I am an innocent man.

Fiddler

APRIL 31, 1985, the O'Neil brothers set out on another halibut adventure. We were fishing on the thirty-eight-foot fishing vessel *Fiddler*, a beautiful boat Dennis had built for his fishing ventures. The halibut openings had been reduced to just one or two days for the whole year. These openings were known as the "derby days." Basically, any boat that floated would go on these halibut openings and attempt to catch fish.

Safety was a major problem with the derby days. The halibut opening date would be posted, and the date was final. The safety problem was due to the very realistic possibility of bad weather. Halibut fishing was a big part of the fisherman's income, and if there was a storm the day of the opening, so be it. The boats were going to fish, and safety concerns were swept aside. It was a necessity to fish. There was one chance to fish halibut for the entire year—often one twenty-four-hour period. As you can imagine, during the derby days there were many sunken boats and tragic endings.

Due to major safety factors, a need for better control of halibut stocks, and many other factors I won't discuss here, the halibut fishery has undergone major changes. In 1985, the National Marine Fishery Service adopted an individual fishing quota (IFQ) program. Each skipper was allotted a quota, or certain amount of pounds, based on their recorded catch during the qualifying years in the late eighties and early nineties. There were many benefits to the new IFQ program. With this new management system, the skippers would now have seven or eight months to catch their IFQs, so they would no longer have to go out when the weather was a safety concern. This would keep fresh fish on the market most of the year. On the downside, the new management system created bad feelings and lost friendships between some skippers and crews. Skippers were rewarded IFQs but crew members, some who had been working on the boat for years and years, received zero. They would have to buy IFQs from a skipper. I am just scratching the surface of the complicated IFQ program. All the pros and cons, who's to blame for declining stocks of halibut, etc., could be a long (and probably boring) book in itself.

On this one-day halibut opening, our dad had come along to go fishing with his boys. It was his first trip, and one he would always remember. How many dads get to go on a commercial fishing halibut trip with their sons? He was so excited. Dad was bragging about the rain gear he had bought for the trip. "Top and bottom, only $29.99, and you boys pay $50 or $60 just for the bottom?" He was so proud of his stylish, lightweight gear he'd bought—an absolute steal from the Bargain Cave. We just smiled and nodded, both thinking the same thing: *Looks like something you'd take the dog for a walk in.* Bargain Cave…that's the rack of cheap stuff that almost no one will buy… well, almost no one.

We began baiting the last of our gear before noon. The weather was mixed rain and snow and fifteen- to twenty-knot winds. Dad was complaining about how cold he was. Dennis and I were toasty warm, working in our overpriced, heavy, stiff raingear. We both saw it at the same time. Dad's Bargain Cave pants were torn from the crack of his ass to the heel of his cheap boots. Dennis and I smiled at each other, and while trying his best not to giggle, Dennis said, "How's that *super* rain gear doing for you, Dad?"

"Well," Dad said, "it feels comfortable, but jeez it's cold out here!" Dennis looked at me and we just lost it. The rear of Dad's pants was flapping in the wind, but he was standing by his fine purchase. He knew something was up when he realized his two sons were giggling like a couple of schoolgirls at him. He started feeling the area where a draft was present, and soon realized why he was freezing his ass off. His $29.99 outfit didn't even make it to the noon opening of the halibut trip. If the price is too good to be true, well, it probably is. Lucky for Dad, there was an extra set of overpriced, thick, stiff old raingear on the boat.

At noon, we were setting out halibut gear. Hook after baited hook, connected to a mainline, began their descent to the bottom of the ocean. By the time we were finished setting gear, there would be over three thousand baited hooks resting on the bottom waiting for halibut to latch on. After letting our gear soak for a short six hours, we began hauling it in. Fish after fish began coming aboard. Seven, eight, nine, ten fish came in a row. This was fishing like we'd never seen! We had hit the mother lode! By midnight it was obvious we needed to go unload our fish to a tender (a bigger boat that would buy the fish from us). At the rate we were catching fish, there was no way we would be able to hold all the fish on the F/V *Fiddler*. In the eighties, when you delivered to a tender, your catch was weighed and you were paid on the spot in one hundred dollar bills.

After our delivery, cash in hand, we headed right back to our gear to begin hauling again. It was around two or three o'clock in the morning, and the season would close at noon. There was definitely no time for sleep. We needed to get the gear and fish on board before noon. Dennis was at the roller bringing fish aboard, I was dressing and icing as fast as possible, and Dad was running around helping out wherever he could and saying, "*JEEZ!*" a lot.

The fishing didn't slow down. It got even better. Not only were there lots of fish, the fish were all really nice sized. Sixty to eighty pounders were coming over the rail on a regular basis. By ten o'clock in the morning, the *Fiddler*'s fish holds below deck were plugged. The fish from our last set would have to go on the deck. Another hour and a half of hauling, and we had all of our gear on the boat, plus a healthy deck load of halibut. The F/V *Fiddler* was full, and Dad and the boys were happy! It was going to be a good day, even if we were only getting about fifty cents a pound for one of the best-eating fish in the world. Fifty cents a pound is tough to believe, when the price for the fishermen today is more like six to eight dollars a pound. The IFQ program definitely has a major role in the increased prices of halibut.

Dennis headed the *Fiddler* toward home. I continued dressing the last of the halibut and making sure things were secure on deck. The weather was cool, and we were getting occasional snow squalls, but the seas were not bad. About two hours into our trip home, the weather took a turn for the worse. We were in a very heavy tidal area. The wind was blowing against the current, causing the seas to build by the minute. The winds would increase in force every time a snow squall would come through. I would guess the wind was an average of twenty to twenty-five knots out of the southeast. When a snow squall would come through, the intensity would increase to thirty-five knots (kt.=1.2 mph). Big winds and heavy tidal currents going in opposite directions, make for big seas. And it's amazing how fast it happens.

I remained on the back deck making sure that the scuppers (drain openings on deck) remained clear, so the water would continually drain off the deck. The seas continued to build, and the *Fiddler* was struggling to push through the oncoming seas. The boat was making slow progress bucking into the steep and close-together waves. I had a five-gallon bucket and was scooping water and throwing it back into the seas whenever a wave would crest over a corner of the stern. I became busier and busier, trying to keep the scuppers free of incoming water.

At one point, I wasn't sure what happened, but the *Fiddler* almost came to a stop for a few seconds. I thought Dennis was slowing down for a big wave, but he had run straight into a steep one. The wave stalled our forward momentum for a second. I looked back and watched a steep wave come curling over the stern of the boat. I'll never forget the sight of that wave as long as I live. I held out my bucket as if I was going to catch it. The wave went right over my head and knocked me down. The stern of the *Fiddler* was suddenly filled with water, and the scuppers had no chance of keeping up and draining this much water. There was no doubt in my mind; we were going down. Dennis had his hands full up front. He had felt the loss of speed too, but he had no idea what the situation was on the stern end of the boat.

I was wading toward the cabin door when Dad took a peek through the window. When he looked out and saw me wading through the water on the deck, his face had *holy shit* written all over it, and so did mine. Dennis gave the *Fiddler* full throttle in a desperate attempt to shed the water from the stern. But it was no use. The stern kept dropping further into the seas. I made my way to the flying bridge, where the three survival suits were stored. It's amazing how fast a guy can get into a suit when he has to.

Dennis made a radio call to a boat about a mile ahead of us when he realized the inevitable. We were going into the water. The *Fiddler's* stern was almost under and the pitch of the bow was getting steeper and steeper. The angle of the boat made the task of getting our survival suits on a bit tricky, but knowing they could make the difference between living or dying made them go on very quickly. The three of us made a pact. We were going into the water together, arm in arm, and *no one lets go*. Just before we took the plunge, Dennis made one final run into the cabin and was back in a few seconds. There was no time to ask, so I just assumed he had run back to make a final call on the radio to let them know we were going in.

Arm in arm, hand in hand, we went into the water, connected as one. The *Fiddler* was just about to fall stern first en route to the bottom of Frederick Sound. We wanted to be a good distance away from the boat in case a vacuum scenario was created when the *Fiddler* went down.

The three of us were quickly swept away from the boat. I can't describe the feeling looking back at just the bow of the *Fiddler* poking out of the water. *Sickening* is the only word I can think of.

We laid our heads back and let the survival suits do their job keeping us afloat. A wave would break over us, and we would pop right back up, arm in arm. Within thirty minutes, the F/V *Summer Breeze*, a forty-foot aluminum, was in our sights. It was the boat Dennis had called on the radio with our location. Mark Jensen was the captain, and Dave Somerville was his mate on this halibut trip. They both were good friends of ours. We were doing some arm waving as Mark got closer. He was a distance off, zigging and zagging looking for us. We would be on top of a wave and there he would be, and then down the wave, and the *Summer Breeze* would disappear again. We all watched Mark drive by us hoping, hoping, he had seen us and was just going by to set up his approach.

Sure enough, the *Summer Breeze* began to turn back toward us. Mark and Dave had seen us. Mark did a perfect job maneuvering the boat close to us. We didn't know if all three of us were going to get over the side of the boat on the first pass. I was pretty positive I would make it, and Dennis had no doubt he was going to make it, but we were not overconfident Dad would make it. Dad just needed to hang on to the rail of the boat, and we would all pull him in. That was our plan.

The *Summer Breeze* maneuvered alongside the three of us. I climbed over the side and Dennis climbed over the stern corner. Dad was hanging on to the rail as we had discussed. I grabbed him under one armpit and Dennis grabbed him under the other armpit. We gave poor 150-pound, soaking-wet Dad a swift adrenaline lift. He went shooting out of the water like a penguin jumping on the rocks with a great white shark on his ass. Dad went flying up and over the rail. When he hit the deck, he landed on a halibut, squirted off it, and slid right into an aluminum drum with his head. Poor Dad staggered to his feet still not sure what the hell just happened.

We all got inside and out of our survival suits. Dad got the nice new gash on his head bandaged up. We were all safe. We would never be able to thank Mark and Dave enough for rescuing us.

Mark headed the *Summer Breeze* toward a calm bay where we could get picked up by a floatplane and fly us home to Petersburg. About an hour had gone by, and hardly a word had been spoken. I felt so bad for my brother. His pride and joy that he had built was gone…

forever. I could have cared less about the money we lost in all that halibut. I just was sick for my brother.

Finally, after a long period of silence, good ol' Dad broke the silence. It went like this, "Hey, Skipper Mark, what's the chance of getting a little sip of something real strong?" Mark quickly set Dad up with a glass of Crown Royal. Dad, with his bloody head continued, "Jesus Christ, I thought I was going to die! Then all of a sudden, we see you coming to save us. I thought, *I'm not going to die*, then the next thing you know you go right on by us. Jesus Christ, I *am* going to die, and then you turned to come pick us up, and then I knew I was going to live!" Dad took a big sip of his beverage and continued. "Then you pull alongside us and I knew I was going to make it, and then my god damned boys jerked me over the rail and damn near killed my ass!"

The boat went instantly from silence to uncontrollable laughter. We were almost peeing our pants. I feel bad for Dave. I'm pretty sure he was out on deck dressing fish and missed Dad's version of the story. How could we all be uncontrollably giggling like a bunch of girls after we just lost a beautiful boat and almost our lives? I guess in Dad's weird way, he'd put it into perspective. We all had our lives, and it was great to be alive!

An hour later, we had entered the calm shelter of a bay and boarded our floatplane. On our flight back, I asked Dennis why he had made the last second dash into the cabin before we went into the water. "Well," he said, "I just couldn't let the cash we had received from the tender go to the bottom."

It was a bumpy flight back. The pilot decided to take a short cut back to shave off a little time. He entered Portage Bay and was just about committed to flying through a narrow passage through Petersburg Creek, when a black snow squall hit us. All landmarks were gone. To say the least, the pucker-factor was high. Dad spoke to break the silence again, "*Jeez*, you've got to be kidding me!"

We were all thinking the same thing. I was actually more afraid now than when we first went in the water. We had zero control of what was going to happen in this plane. At least we had had a fighting chance in our survival suits. The experienced pilot knew right where he was and banked hard and back out of the snow squall. We were going to make it yet.

After landing at the floatplane dock, we were met by Dennis's wife, Heather, and Dad's new wife, Peggy. My wife, Cheryl, was in Oregon about to have our first child. We all hugged and began walking down the long airplane ramp to Heather's car. It was a cold, cold walk. There was three feet of wet snow and slush on the ground, and the three amigos had only socks on. We'd taken our boots off to get into our survival suits.

It was a lonely house when I got home. Cheryl had been in my thoughts all day. I needed to call her before she heard the news secondhand. After a hot shower, I made the call. Telling her what had happened was a bit tougher than anticipated. There were a few pauses to collect my emotions when giving her the details of our ordeal. I told her I would be on the next plane out of Petersburg and should be in Portland around 8:30 p.m. I received a phone call less than twenty-four hours later. I was a proud father of a new baby girl. Julie Kay O'Neil was born at 7:58 p.m. on May 2, 1985. I guess I must have sped up the delivery, as our little girl arrived ten days early. That evening, after finally arriving in Portland, I got to give my wife the biggest, longest hug and hold my new little daughter, Julie Kay. Life was good.

There were four boats that went down on May 1, 1985, but to my knowledge no lives were lost. A couple of months later, a second one-day halibut opening was announced. A friend Mike Schwartz offered Dennis his forty-seven-foot F/V *Glacier Spirit* to fish the opening. It was just going to be Dennis and me on the boat, but Dad insisted he was going too. We both knew he didn't want to step foot on that boat. Dad would not take no for an answer. We both know why he went. He wanted to show us that he had complete confidence in his boys. This meant a lot to Dennis and me and always will. We had a good trip with no extra excitement. Shortly after that season, Dad moved to

Palm Springs, California, with Peggy and has been there ever since.

It took about four years for Dennis to completely rebound from the *Fiddler* sinking. Now, in addition to halibut fishing, he was crabbing, salmon gill-netting, black cod fishing, and shrimping. I continued fishing the halibut derby days with my brother until the new IFQ program was implemented ten years later.

Dad sitting on deck load of halibut...

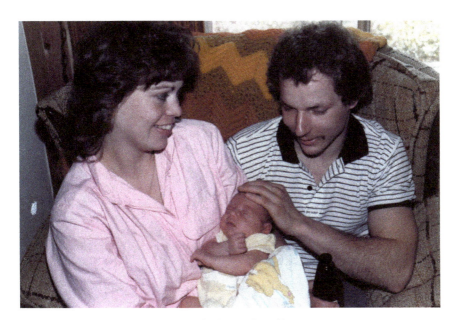

Our new baby girl, Julie Kay

Driving in Circles

WE HEADED OUT on Dennis's new boat, the F/V *Vulcan* on May 1, 1987, for another big twenty-four-hour halibut opening. The *Vulcan* was a very seaworthy forty-foot flush-deck aluminum boat. The weather forecast was light winds and calm seas for the next few days. With such a great weather forecast, Dennis decided to go to the open ocean on this trip and hopefully get into some good fishing. Our normal fishing grounds had not produced as well as they had in the previous years, so we both agreed to take the gamble and try the big open waters.

We finally arrived after a long fifteen-hour run. We had made it with just two hours to spare before the twenty-four-hour halibut opener. The weatherman was right—light and variable winds and calm seas. The ocean was calm except for the big, slow, lazy ocean waves. As the boat slowly rose to the top of each wave, you could see endless miles of ocean with no land in sight. Slowly, the boat would gently drop down the wave, and our view would be gone until we ascended to the top of the next wave. It was an eerie feeling to be so far from the safety of land.

We had both taken our seasick pills. The ocean was calm, but the slow rolling waves and no landmarks were perfect conditions to make you sick. If you've ever been seasick, you know it's not fun to say the least, and it can last for a day, two days, and even a week. If you waited until you were sick to take your seasick pill, it was too late. Once you get seasick, there is no pill that's going to miraculously cure you. You end up puking your guts out until you have nothing left to donate to the sea. We'd both been seasick on occasions and made sure we took our pills long before we reached the ocean swells.

Noon finally came, and with it, the beginning of another twenty-four-hour derby day halibut opening. Within three and a half hours, we had all of our gear set. We let the gear soak for about four hours to give the halibut a chance to get on our hooks—four hours of anticipation. Did we set our gear on some fish? Was our gamble worth it? All we could do was hope, pray, and beg that we set our hooks in the right area.

With the gear all set, now would have been a good time to get a four-hour nap, but there was just too much anticipation and excitement for sleep. Three and a half hours later, we began hauling our first set, both of us staring down into the water watching for signs of life as our hydraulics steadily brought our long lines full of hooks to the surface. First hook, empty; second hook, empty; third hook, *yes*—a nice halibut! The long line was very active, jerking and moving side to side. It was obvious there were a lot more lively halibut to come. Dennis continued gaffing and bringing fish aboard, and I began dressing our catch. It looked like the O'Neil brothers' gamble had paid off. We'd hit the jackpot—lots of fish and perfect weather conditions. It just couldn't get any better! Dennis yelled, "Dan, you better grab a gaff and come over here. I think there's something big coming up!" I grabbed a gaff and ran over to give Dennis a hand. The line was slowly swaying side to side. Usually, when the long line makes slow long side-to-side movements, you have something large coming. Hopefully this was a big butt, and not a skate or a shark. Slowly, a large shadow began to appear. "Holy crap!" It was a monster butt. She was lying there just as docile as could be. This fish looked to be spent, and we both agreed we could bring her aboard. The other option we had was to go in the cabin, get the pistol, and shoot the fish first, and then bring it aboard. Looking at this tame fish, it didn't seem necessary to take the extra time to get the gun. This halibut was already pooped out.

Dennis bringing fish aboard

Guess what? We were wrong! Should have gotten the gun. We both got on the gunnel of the boat to get more leverage, Dennis sunk his gaff in the fish's head, and I sunk mine next to his. We both leaned back and pulled with everything we had. The fish was almost at its pivot point on the gunnel. One last big pull and the gentle giant came over the side. About the time the halibut was cresting over the gunnel, all hell broke loose. Our docile, gentle giant woke up. As the halibut fell to the deck, I was able to get my gaff free from the fish. Dennis couldn't get his gaff loose from the wild, out-of-control fish. The last thing that you want to do is leave a gaff hook in a wild fish. Bad things can happen.

The two-hundred-fifty-pound fish was twisting brother Dennis every which way but loose, and he couldn't hang on to his gaff hook any longer. Finally, with eyes wide, Dennis yelled, "Get out of the way, *loose gaff!*" He let go of the gaff in the wild fish. The halibut bucked her head, and the gaff hook catapulted up into the air. The hook landed with the point facing down on the top of Dennis's boot. Dennis bent over to grab the gaff off his boot, and just as he was about to touch the hook, the halibut flopped in the air and thrust its two-hundred-fifty-pound body onto the back of the gaff. I couldn't believe what I'd just seen. The fish had sunk that gaff hook straight into Dennis's foot!

My brother's face instantly turned pale white. "How bad is it?" I asked.

He could barely talk. "It's all the way through my foot!"

"No." Dennis lifted his foot, and the tip of the rusty gaff hook was coming out the bottom of his boot. I immediately went pasty pale white. I couldn't believe my eyes. I almost hurled.

Dennis bent over and yanked the nasty hook out. We went inside the cabin to pull the boot off. When I pulled Dennis's boot off, we realized just how serious this wound was. Blood was squirting everywhere. All Dennis could say was, "Can you believe this? I've really messed up this opening!" He had a possibly life-threatening wound, and all he was worried about was catching a bunch of stupid halibut! I explained the big picture to him. We did not need to worry about the damn opening right now. We desperately needed to stop the bleeding.

As I applied pressure to the bottom of his foot, the blood was forced to gush out the top of the foot. It squirted to the ceiling. That's when Dennis finally realized, "Wow, this is pretty serious." We applied pressure on both sides of his foot, but the wound continued to bleed heavily. Dennis continued to put direct pressure on his foot, and I began applying pressure above his ankle. Finally, we were able to slow the bleeding to a slow ooze. After pouring peroxide on his foot, we plugged up his swelling wound with some antiseptic cream. Then we wrapped his foot the best we could, but it was growing by the minute. Dennis took a few Tylenol, sat in his captain's chair, and got his foot elevated. He was as comfortable as he was going to get. There really wasn't much more to do except call a plane to come get him, and he was adamantly against that idea. We had pretty much stopped the bleeding, and it looked as if the injury was not life threatening.

In order to get the F/V *Vulcan* headed for home, I needed to haul halibut gear as fast as possible so that Dennis could get some real medical attention. We still had the majority of our gear in the water, so it was going to take me all night and part of the morning to get all of the gear back on the boat. I left Dennis in the cabin and headed out to begin hauling gear.

The first thing I did was take out some frustrations on "Mrs. Docile," halibut. I gave her about twenty-five cracks to the head with a size 34 aluminum baseball bat. Once that was taken care of, I began hauling gear.

The fishing remained good. The bad part of this good fishing was that it was slowing down getting the gear back on the boat. I was gaffing the halibut one after another and pulling them directly into the fish hold, uncleaned. I would have to deal with the dressing later. The larger halibut were kicking my ass, but they were coming over the gunnel. It is amazing what a little adrenaline can do.

After about four hours of fishing, Dennis hobbled out to give me a hand. He had made a homemade shoe for his now huge foot. He'd basically just cut the top of his boot out so he could get his swollen foot into it. Dennis propped himself next to the hydraulic valve and ran the hydraulics for me. This was a huge help. Now we could keep the fish coming aboard at a much faster pace. Thank God, we didn't hook into any more monster fish. When a big halibut did come up, it was an automatic bullet to the head. If we had shot our docile gentle giant, we would not have been in this predicament in the first place.

Dennis remained on the deck trying to help me the best he could. He helped me break a few big fish over the rail, balancing on his good foot. The gear and fish kept coming aboard at a good pace. By 4:00 a.m. the last hook and halibut were on board, and our fish holds were just about full. We had done it! There was still eight hours until the end of the opening, but that was the last thing on our minds. Dennis got in his captain's chair, put his foot up on the dash, and headed the F/V *Vulcan* toward home. He was a sore sight, and his foot was one plain-ass, swollen, disgusting, ungodly mess!

My work was just beginning. I had about nine thousand pounds of halibut to dress! The first trick was to get the undressed fish out of the fish holds so I could clean them. Believe me, they went down into the hold a lot easier than they came up out of the hold.

After about three hours of gutting halibut, I felt the boat going over some waves. I looked up to realize that we were going over our own boat waves. Dennis was driving the boat in circles. Hell, Dennis was asleep! No one was driving at all. I ran into the cabin and yelled and gave him a couple of shakes, "Wake up, you're going in circles!"

"Yeah, yeah, right, I'm okay," he mumbled. Back to the deck I went…clean, clean, clean. I had only just begun. Over the next few hours, it became a common occurrence to go in circles. I would yell at the top of my lungs from the back deck, and the boat would slowly get back on the right course. We were definitely taking the long way home!

By 4:00 p.m. we were finally pulling into Petersburg. I had finished cleaning the last and final halibut just before we pulled into our slip. Now I knew why my damn brother was going in circles. He wanted to give me a little extra time so I could finish the job.

All turned out well for Dennis. The rusty gaff went right between two bones. A tetanus shot, and some antibiotics, and Dennis was doing another fishery within a week. I received a much larger crew share for that trip, and I guess I deserved it. It's always nice working for a fair skipper, not to mention a special brother.

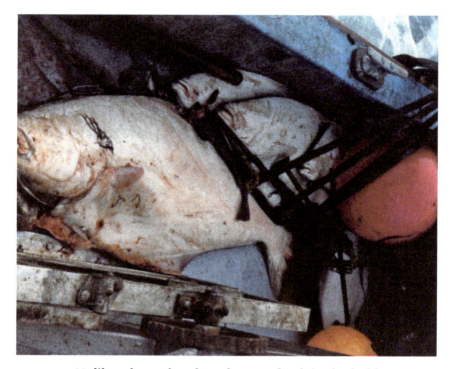

Halibut dressed and ready to go back in the hold

My Goal

FROM MY TODDLER years on up to my twilight years, I have always been a fanatic when it comes to fishing. Through the years I've done both sport and commercial fishing. When I was growing up, people always asked me what I wanted to do when I grew up. The answer was always the same…fish!

I graduated from high school in Petersburg, Alaska, in 1978, and went to college for a couple of years. Basically, the only reason I went to college was because I loved to wrestle and had been offered a wrestling scholarship at Mount Hood Community College in Oregon. I met the love of my life, Cheryl, while attending college. Cheryl came back to Petersburg with me after college. We married two years later and began our wonderful life together. I worked for Alaska Airlines and did some commercial halibut and salmon fishing on the side to get by.

Life was good and I liked my job, but I didn't love it. What I really wanted, my dream job, was to sport fish for a living. I wanted to take fishing enthusiasts out sport fishing and sightseeing and get paid for it. To do this, I would need a guide's charter license. To get this license, I would need to pass a US Coast Guard examination. I researched what I would be tested on, and in 1990, after a couple of attempts, passed the exam. I continued working for Alaska Airlines and also began building my sport fishing business, Secret Cove Charters.

Cheryl and myself

It didn't take long to figure out that if I was going to make it in the charter business, I would need to establish some parameters. I had to learn to accept the fact that you don't catch fish every time. Just because I was getting money for my services, didn't guarantee there would be fish at the end of the day. I had to face the hard reality that there would be days when the fish were not around or were "on vacation." The thought of bringing my customers home with nothing to show for the day, and collecting money from them, was really a tough one for me to swallow. My clients would have to wave the white surrender flag and say, "Dan, you have done your best, you can't make them bite." Surrendering was, and still is, the toughest part of chartering for me. When skunk days or very slow fishing days happened, I would have my clients show up an hour earlier for the boat the next morning. Instead of 5:00 a.m., we would start at 4:00 a.m. We would generally start fishing salmon in the morning and switch to halibut in the early afternoon, and then back to salmon in the late afternoon.

After a long day of fishing, it was normally time to clean, fillet, and package the client's fish, then clean the boat and get it ready for the next morning. By the time my day ended it would be nine or ten at night. I was working dark to dark. I was doing charters in the morning before work at Alaska Airlines, and evening charters after I got off work at Alaska Airlines. I was working myself to the bone, literally to the bone.

Cheryl finally put her foot down, "Dan, you're tired. You've lost about twenty pounds. You look like a starving Ethiopian. Something has got to change." Yes, she was right. If I was going to be in the business for the long run, I needed to establish boundaries and more manageable working hours. If it was a slow day, I could put in an extra hour of fishing, but I could not be putting in an extra four or five. I

DROPPING MY LINES

was learning to accept that if I did my best, tried my hardest, and still came up empty-handed, that was okay.

Now that I had a schedule, Cheryl and I were actually able to spend some quality time together. Sport fishing for a living was definitely not as easy as I'd thought. As the years went on, Cheryl and I have built Secret Cove Charters into a very successful business. What do you want to do when you grow up? The answer is…fish, and fifty years later I'm still doing the job I love. When I see new young guides getting into the business, I have to smile a little. It's not going to be quite as easy as they think it is. Go out, catch fish, and come home. What's so hard about that? I smile. They might make it in this business, and then again there's a good chance they won't.

THE CHARTER SKIPPER'S PROMISE…

MY GOAL

Toddler or Elder. Fishing is always fun!

Eyeball

ON MAY 2, 1985, Cheryl gave birth to our first bundle of joy, Julie Kay. Two years later, on May 14, 1987, she gave birth to our son, Scott William. It didn't take long 'til they both had nicknames. Scott came by the name of The Destroyer, and Julie was to be known as The Informer. They both have my fishing genes, and both absolutely love to fish. When a day off from chartering comes, the F/V *Julie Kay* usually goes on family fishing trips.

Scott grew up fishing off the docks. Like me, he also had to get a schedule! Our little seven-year-old would bring his bucket, tackle box, and fishing pole down to the dock and fish for herring and his favorite, Dolly Varden trout, all day long. I would normally return from a charter around four or five in the afternoon, and he would take time from his busy fishing schedule to come and meet the boat. He was always excited to see what Dad's clients had caught that day. My clients got the biggest kick out of him; this little guy in his life jacket trying so hard to help Dad.

Scott didn't get the handle, The Destroyer, for nothing. He had a little trick he loved to play on my clients. Usually, if there was a woman in the group, she would be his victim. I would get the fish out of the boat and bring them about twenty feet down the dock to a cleaning table, as well as Scott's Dolly Varden hot spot. Usually, I would begin cleaning salmon, and then I would work on halibut. While I cleaned fish, Scott would be entertaining my clients by fishing for Dollies. They'd be all smiles watching how excited he would get when he'd catch one or lose one.

EYEBALL

Now that he had their undivided attention, he would do his "trick." He would quit fishing and go over to the biggest halibut we had caught that day. Then Scott would take out his dull little pocketknife and very carefully perform a surgery on the fish's eye. Finally, he would have the halibut's eyeball detached and in his slimy little hand. No one was watching me clean fish anymore. All eyes were on The Destroyer. He would stand up and show everyone the big halibut eyeball (which really are huge). Soon he'd have some poor unsuspecting lady looking closely at the eyeball in his little hand. Scott would hold the big eyeball up a little higher so the poor, unsuspecting lady could get a better look. That's when he'd do it. He would begin squeezing the eyeball until it went *pop*, followed by the woman's scream. Eyeball juice had gone everywhere, all over her, and anyone trying to get a closer look. Scott would be rolling on the dock laughing. He thought this trick was hilarious. It really was funny! Now my clients knew where he got his nickname.

The Destroyer

The Three Youngsters Go Fishing

ON MANY OCCASIONS, my clients would request Scott or Julie go with us on a charter. I would often bring one of them, but *never* both. I was getting paid to take people fishing. I didn't want to have to pay them for babysitting. Scott had a way of finagling his way onto the boat quite often.

On one particular occasion, I had Max, better known as "The Judge," and his brother Earl in town to go halibut fishing. The brothers had fished with me before, and they had also become good buddies with Mr. Scott. We were going halibut fishing in the morning, and the brothers asked me if Scott could go along on the trip. I told them I'd think about it, but I didn't want anything to get in the way of their charter. So I informed them, "They don't call him The Destroyer because he's an angel!" I gave Scott the news that night. He pleaded and begged and, as usual, I gave in. Scott was going to get to go halibut fishing with The Judge and his brother Earl.

The Judge was in his late seventies, and his brother Earl was in his early eighties. It was always a quick and fun fishing trip with these two. They liked to leave the dock late and return early. They were the perfect charter, and it worked out great to take The Destroyer along.

On the way to the boat, The Judge and Scott were already making bets. Before we even got to the boat, Scott asked me for five dollars for the bet. The Judge, Earl, and Scott had a five-dollar bet on the biggest fish. They insisted Scott was going to be one of my clients today, and he would be fishing his own pole. If he caught the biggest fish, he would be taking home the loot. What could I say? "Okay, it's your trip."

It was another beautiful calm day on the water. Within an hour I had the boat anchored on the halibut hole. My little boy and the two spring chickens lowered their lines to the bottom.

It didn't take long for the boys to start hooking halibut. We were all having an absolute ball. Watching The Judge and Earl reeling in halibut was always entertaining. The pole would never come out of the pole holder. They would just sit in their chairs and keep winding on their reel (poor reel). If the fish was a decent-sized one, this method would really put the reel and pole holder to the test.

Most of the fish being caught were small, so we chose to release them so they could all continue fishing. Scott was having a great time being part of the group, and he was catching and releasing along with his two new buddies.

After a while, The Judge landed a fifty-pound butt, and it looked as though he was going to take the pot. I was just about to call it a day when The Destroyer yelled, "I've got a big one on, Dad!" Sure enough, he did. The rod was doubled over, and his line was disappearing off the reel.

I said, "Judge, Earl, grab that pole. It's a big one!"

They both looked at me like I was crazy. "That's Scott's pole. We want Scott to reel it in." They would have it no other way, period. They were paying for the entire boat, and they wanted to see my son catch a big fish. Scott's eyes were the size of halibut eyes. "It's okay," they said, "it's your fish."

THE THREE YOUNGSTERS GO FISHING

Scott fighting his fish

Scott went to work on his halibut. First, he started reeling with the pole in the holder but wasn't making much progress. I asked The Judge to help Scott get the pole out of the holder and help him pump the rod up so Scott could reel as he let the pole back down each time. I just stood back laughing and giving directions. Pretty soon, Earl was in on the action too. What a sight! Two old farts lifting the rod, and little Destroyer reeling for all his fifty-pound self was worth. Scott had the butt of the rod sandwiched between his legs. His manhood was really taking a beating! Finally, the worn-out boys got the fish to the top. The fish was as tired as the fishermen. If that fish could have waved a white flag, I think it would have. About five whacks over the head with my size 34 aluminum baseball bat, and, with the help of The Judge, over the side and in the boat the big fish came. Scott, with a little help, had caught a hundred-twenty-five-pound halibut. At seven years old, this was the highlight of his life!

On the way back to town, The Judge and Earl each paid Scott his five bucks. While walking up the dock, The Judge asked Scott if he could have a five-dollar loan. The Destroyer looked him right in the eye and said, "Your five dollars is in my pocket and that's where it's gonna stay!"

That evening Scott received a phone call from The Judge. When Scott hung up the phone he let out a big "Yes!" He said, "I've got a charter tomorrow!"

I said, "What do you mean *you* have a charter?"

"The Judge and Earl have hired me to take them Dolly Varden fishing on the docks tomorrow! I'm meeting them at the dock at nine o'clock!"

All Cheryl and I could say was, "O...kay...I guess."

The Judge and Earl had no idea what they were in for. The next morning Scott headed off with his pole and bucket to meet up with his clients. I had the day off, and I was going to stay as far away from the docks as possible! Scott returned home from the big Dolly Varden dock charter around 1:00 p.m. He was all jacked up. "Twenty dollars! Twenty dollars!" The Judge and Earl had created a Destroyer-monster. "It was the best fishing ever. We caught big ones and huge ones! Earl and The Judge had a blast, Dad!"

Later that evening, I got a call from The Judge. He thanked me for such a great trip and told me how much he enjoyed Scott. I asked how the big charter with The Destroyer went. He had a little different story than Scott! "Well, it was exciting. Earl had a big one break his line and I lost one. Scott was giving us pointers, but I guess we were lousy students. Scott showed us the art of hooking and landing a Dolly Varden. He showed it to us over and over again. Dan, you need to teach Scott that the customer is supposed to catch the fish, not the guide!" He laughed and laughed and said he'd see me again next year and that he was planning another Dolly Varden trip too, if Scott's calendar wasn't full...

Three youngsters and their catch

M&Ms

A FEW YEARS later, The Judge and Earl returned. They had definitely aged but still had the fishing fever and wanted just one more fishing experience in Petersburg. I had them chartered for two days. The first day we fished for halibut. They just wanted to catch a couple of medium-sized fish. They had caught their share of larger fish in the past, and we all knew that a big halibut would be too much for them to handle. At their age, they just wanted to be out on the water enjoying the scenery while doing a little fishing. Most of all, they just wanted to sit around and tell stories of the past. That's one of the things I love about chartering…all the great, interesting people and their stories.

On the first day, Earl and The Judge each caught and released multiple halibut before keeping two thirty pounders. They were pretty exhausted, so we called it a short day and headed home. The next day I suggested trying something different. Instead of the regular old halibut trip, I said, "Let's go after king salmon." They had never caught a king, and I thought a king on the end of a limber rod might get the old blood moving again.

We fished at Blind Slough, about a forty-minute boat ride from town. It was a rainy, ugly Southeast Alaska day. I explained to the brothers that this was nothing like halibut fishing. When a king hits, you quickly have to get the pole out of the holder. The drag is set so the fish can run and not break a line. He will turn and run at you, and that's when you need to reel as fast as you can. They both just looked at me, mouths open. "Dan," said The Judge, "I thought you said this was easier than halibut fishing?" It was easier physically, yet harder to actually land the fish.

The lines went in the water and it happened quickly. The Judge's rod took a sudden dive, and the line started peeling off the reel. He looked at me like someone had a finger up his butt! He was in panic mode. I yelled, "Grab it, Judge!"

He managed the rod out of its holder and just started reeling. It didn't matter if the fish was going away or toward him, as The Judge was reeling as fast as he could. He looked to be in a state of shock—no talking, bug eyes, mouth open, reeling and reeling. This was nothing like fighting a lazy halibut. The old codger had adrenaline working for him. The salmon swam by the boat, and Earl and The Judge could see him. They were both in awe of the beauty and power of the fish. One more run, and The Judge slowly guided the salmon alongside the boat, and into the net he came. The fish was spent. The Judge was spent. He had landed about a thirty-pound king. Earl and The Judge were shaking with excitement.

I will never forget how excited they both were. It was a thrill for me to see The Judge land that fish. Getting a king on and actually landing it was a true dream come true for The Judge. We took some pictures and began trolling again. It was Earl's turn now. Earl, now in his mid-eighties, wasn't quite as quick and agile as his younger brother. Catching a king was going to be a real challenge/miracle for Earl. After witnessing the battle his brother had with his fish, Earl was a bit hesitant, but after some encouragement he was ready to give it a try.

Again, it didn't take long. Earl's rod took a quick bend, but before he could get out of his chair the fish was gone. The fish gods would not be with Earl on this day. He had three more fish on but was outfoxed each time. Earl was a bit wet and cold and decided to go inside the cabin and warm up.

The Judge and I stayed out on deck and talked and watched the rods, hoping, begging Earl would get another chance at a king. Earl sat down inside and was soon sound asleep. About an hour later, the cabin door opened up, and Earl came running, or should I say trying to run. He had his pants unbuttoned and unzipped heading for the side of the boat, yet stopped short. It was too late. Earl had pissed his pants. He had really pissed his pants well. He was wet front and back. Poor Earl was humiliated. I tried to make light of it. "It's okay, Earl. No big deal. Go ahead and clean yourself up. Hell, it's just us guys out here." Earl went back in the cabin, cleaned up a bit, and then came out on deck to air out a bit.

We fished awhile longer while Earl and The Judge swapped stories. I had heard some of the stories a few times, but I still enjoyed them. Then as if this trip didn't already have enough entertainment, Earl decided to one-up himself on his pissing of the pants. Earl slipped his right hand into his soggy right pants pocket and out came a soggy little bag. "Dan, Judge, can I interest you in some M&Ms?" The Judge held his cupped hands out as Earl tried to shake the soggy chocolates in his hands. The only thing holding the M&Ms together was the peanut in the middle. I almost lost my cookies!

Earl looked at me and held out the soggy bag toward me. "Sorry, Earl, I'm going to have to pass." The brothers finished off the rest. Between the smell and the chewing of the soggy M&Ms, I was having a hard time not hurling over the side.

We pulled in the lines and headed home in the smelly cabin of the *Julie Kay*. When I came home that day, I told Cheryl about the M&Ms, and she said, "No way!" Then she paused, looked at me again, and began hysterically laughing. She knew there was no way I could have made a story like that up.

I've stayed away from M&Ms ever since that trip. That was the last fishing trip Earl and The Judge ever made with me. I will never forget them. They really were special and dear friends.

DROPPING MY LINES

Dream Fish

YOU JUST NEVER know what is going happen in the heat of the battle with a fish. This morning, I had Bill and Nancy from Salem, Oregon, on the boat. Bill was a true fisherman. He'd fished for years, and had caught hundreds of salmon, but nothing over twenty pounds. Nancy had never fished, and the only reason she was here was because I wouldn't take Bill out unless I had two paying customers. Bill was in Petersburg, Alaska, and he had to go fishing. He whined to Nancy that she just had to go fishing, and she finally relented.

It was a beautiful morning, and Nancy was in heaven. There was calm water, porpoises, eagles, a bear, and icebergs. If Bill had said, "Dear, would you like to go on a sightseeing trip?" he wouldn't have had to put on his whining baby show to get her on the boat. Sightseeing was great, but fishing started out slow. Bill, being the true salmon fisherman, understood fishing and didn't get discouraged.

It had been hours and hours, and more hours of nothing. Then, out of the blue, *ka-bam,* Nancy's rod bent down into the water, and her thirty-pound test line started screaming off the reel! Bill ran for the pole and grabbed it out of the holder. "I've...um...you've got a fish on, Nancy!" Poor Bill had a death grip on the rod and it took all the power he had to release the rod to his wife.

Nancy took over the rod and Bill began barking out orders. It was definitely a big fish. I had my hands full just trying to get the boat turned to follow the fish before Nancy was out of line. For a non-fisherman, Nancy was doing great. Once I had the boat turned toward the fish, Bill had his wife cranking in the slack line as fast as she could reel.

After twenty minutes of multiple long runs, the king began to tire. Nancy was exhausted but kept battling Bill's once-in-a-lifetime dream fish. Finally, the brute came by the boat but was way out of net's distance. We were all silent except Nancy, "Is it a good sized one, honey?" Bill was still silent. His honey buns had about a fifty-pound-plus king on the end of her line! It was a monster.

Again, the fish came near the boat and didn't like what he saw. That's when shit hit the fan! The big salmon took off on a wicked run. Nancy had just about had it, and being fatigued, she wasn't thinking clearly. In the midst of the big king's run, Nancy let her thumb slip into the level wind reel. It was too late. The power of the running fish quickly had her thumb pinched between the level wind and the side plate of the reel. The harder the fish tried to run, the more pressure it put on Nancy's now bloody thumb.

She was screaming like a newborn baby after he's had his ass slapped. I took a couple small tugs at her mangled thumb, but it was pinned. It was pretty ugly. The thumbnail was split, and she was howling for good reason.

I told Bill I was going to cut the line. I was just trying to save a marriage. Cutting the line was not going to be an option. This was Bill's dream fish! Bill announced, "Nobody's cutting the mother fucking line!"

He grabbed his sweetie's hand and ripped her thumb out of the reel. She was wailing. Bill took the rod and began playing the fish. I got Nancy bandaged up while Bill, who was now in heaven, was fighting the fish of his dreams.

Bill was trying to comfort Nancy while he was having the time of his life. But she wasn't a happy wife. She was obviously thinking that this stupid fish was more important to Bill than her finger. Bill must have been thinking that this was his one and only shot at catching a salmon like this. He'd have a good chance of getting another wife!

Bill almost had the lunker salmon in. Nancy came out of the

DREAM FISH

cabin. "Bill," she says, "I think I'm well enough to catch my fish now."

The smile came off Bill's face instantly. "Honey, are you sure?"

Nancy was a real trooper and pulled the rod away from her husband. A minute later, the tired king salmon made his final trip to the boat, and with a swoop of the net the dream fish was hers. Nancy had caught her first king salmon, a fifty-two pounder! The biggest king Bill had ever seen was brought in by his wife!

For the moment, Nancy had forgotten about her finger. Bill gave his current wife at that time a big hug. Bill later caught a nice king, not quite half the size of Nancy's.

I later took a picture with the couple posing with their fish. I could see a little twinkle in Nancy's eyes. I don't think she had forgotten about Bill being willing to sacrifice her thumb for a stupid fish. Bill would be paying dearly for Nancy's dream fish for a long time.

Beautiful Creatures

THIS MORNING I was taking Eldon, Bert, and their two grandkids fishing and sightseeing. This had become a regular event every early July. The older couple would treat their granddaughter Kandra (nine) and grandson Malin (ten) to an Alaskan vacation year after year.

Eldon and Bert would tow their seventeen-foot skiff behind their truck and arrive in Petersburg on the Alaska State Ferry in early July. They would rent one of Petersburg's local hotel rooms for an entire month. Most of their fishing would be for salmon in the calm waters of the Wrangell Narrows.

Three or four times in July, the group would charter me to go halibut fishing and sightseeing. I would keep an eye on the weather forecasts and pick a nice day for the charter.

After an hour of herring jigging, we were heading thirty to forty miles north of Petersburg. It was about an hour and a half run in the *Julie Kay*. The weather forecast was perfect, and it was flat, calm water and blue skies.

The scenery part would be a given today—a black bear on the beach, bald eagles, porpoises, sea lions, and whales everywhere. I was just zigzagging between pods of humpback whales. I would give the mammoth creatures ample room and shut the engine down so we could watch and listen at a safe distance. Grandpa, Grandma, and grandkids would all be on the back deck taking pictures and filming the unbelievable sights. There's nothing more spectacular than seeing whales breaching and feeding!

BEAUTIFUL CREATURES

Orcas playing

It was always a pleasure to take this group out. The kids were well mannered and very well disciplined. They respected their grandparents and did as they were asked. They always wore life jackets and obeyed my boat rules. It can make a long, nerve-racking day when you have to babysit kids all day. This was not the case with Malin and Kandra. They were a pleasure, and going fishing with Captain Dan had become a highlight of their summers.

After a wonderful morning of whale watching, it was time for everyone's favorite: halibut fishing. Bert had a goal of catching a halibut over one hundred pounds. She had caught lots of halibut in her life but was still looking for a big one. Bert told me that if she ever got a big halibut, she was going to take its ear bones and have earrings made out of them.

I anchored the boat and it wasn't long before the kids were busy cranking in halibut. Often, a little help from Grandpa would be needed. Bert would keep the camcorder rolling for future memories. The scenery part of the trip had been fantastic and soon became even better.

Two enormous sea lions appeared beside the boat. I instructed the kids and grandparents to just let their lines sit on the bottom whether or not there were fish on them. I told them the lions would make a meal out of a halibut if they attempted to bring one up from the bottom. They really didn't believe Captain Dan, but they did as I asked.

I've had many encounters with these beasts, and the outcome is never good. The sea lions were really putting on a show. This was another first for Grandpa, Grandma, and the kids—face-to-face with the stinky-breathed, big-eyed, panting dogs. It was all being added to the tape on Eldon's camcorder. Bert was really enjoying the show. "Just look how fearless of the boat they are. God has blessed us with these beautiful creatures!" I kept quiet and let them all enjoy the moment (thinking to myself, *I'd like to bless them with a size 34 aluminum bat right between the eyes so we could get back to fishing*).

Bert and Eldon were church-going people, and I'd never heard a negative word or, God forbid, a cuss word out of either of them. Malin, on the other hand, would let one slip in his excitement! It was likely something he'd picked up from school, but certainly not from Grandma and Grandpa. Grandpa would have to do some editing on the tape before Mom and Dad would see it!

After forty-five minutes of sea lion entertainment, the big pests moved on and we got back to fishing. The kids were tag teaming a nice thirty-pound halibut. Malin would hold up on the rod, and his sister would crank on the reel. While they were working on their fish, one of the other rods took the slow, big fish bend.

I told Bert to grab the rod. This might be the halibut she was looking for. Bert grabbed the pole, and the line was steadily leaving the reel. Grandpa was laughing and filming at the same time. Malin and Kandra finally got their fish to the top, and I gaffed it and pulled it aboard.

Bert was having a real struggle with her big fish. It had made a couple of long runs, and she was beginning to get some line back. Thirty minutes later, Bert was closing the gap. The fish was slowly coming straight up. She had help now. The grandkids would lift on the rod, and Bert would reel. Grandpa just kept giggling and filming.

Within sixty feet of the boat, the halibut went on another run. The kids and Grandma were all hanging on to the rod. Captain Dan's instructions were, "Never, never, never, let go of your rod." Suddenly, the fish gained incredible power, and the line was smoking off the reel at Mach speed. Instead of the halibut going straight down for the bottom, she was going out to the side.

I realized what was happening. Our cute furry bundles of fun had returned, and they had hold of Bert's big halibut. Soon the line came to the surface, and on the other end were two sea lions chewing on Bert's first hundred-plus-pound halibut. I tightened down the drag and told Bert to pull for all she was worth. Bert was speechless, but did as I asked.

The lions would let go of the fish, and Bert would reel for all she was worth, and then they would grab the fish again and the line would peel off the reel. Grandpa Eldon was still filming the show. The kids were yelling at the lions, "Let go, let Grandma's fish go!"

Finally, the church-going grandma ended her silence. "Why, these fifthly, no good, dirty rotten, sons of bitches! You God-damned bastards give me my fish!"

DROPPING MY LINES

Grandpa was shaking and taping. Grandma Bert was pissed! This was a side of her I'd never seen. Bert would pull as hard as she could, and the cuddly critters would let go. Then she'd start pumping and reeling as fast as possible, until they'd grab the fish again. Finally, Bert broke the halibut free of the lions again. This time there was no resistance from the sea lions. We were all yelling, "Reel, reel, reel!"

Bert got the fish all the way to the boat. Well, she got the fish's head to the boat. The sea lions had taken the entire fish…all but the head. Grandma had caught the head of her one hundred-pound halibut. Poor Bert was pooped and pissed. "Those God-damn, no good, sons of bitches," is all she could say. No doubt God had made a mistake when it came to sea lions.

On the trip back to town, I told the story of one of my best buddies, Troy, almost getting pulled in the water by a huge sea lion. He was unloading halibut after a commercial halibut trip. He was sitting on the side of the boat, waiting for the empty tote to be dropped back down to the deck so it could be filled with fish. Troy was just relaxing fifteen feet above the water, and suddenly something grabbed him by the ass. It was all he could do to avoid being pulled into the water. A sea lion had jumped out of the water and clamped down on Troy's butt! Thank God Troy is a big man, or surely, he would have been pulled in the water. The sea lion tore right through his rain pants and tore his butt wide open. The lion was later put down by the Fish and Game. Troy, or as I like to call him, my half-ass friend, received multiple stiches in his butt! At the end of my story, the kids gave me the, "I don't believe you, Captain Dan" look.

After getting back to the dock, I began digging Bert's ear bones out of what was left of her one-hundred-pound halibut. She could still have earrings made. While I worked on getting the little white ear bones out of the halibut's head, my half-ass friend, Troy, came walking by. He walked over and I introduced him, and he told my crew that the story was in fact true. He even did one better and turned around and dropped his pants to show a bare ass with one huge sea lion bite on his left cheek. All eyes were on Troy's shapely formed ass! Wide-eyed, Malin stammered, "Holy shit! Captain Dan was telling the truth!" Grandpa still had the camera rolling. What a perfect end to his movie.

A year later, Bert finally got her 100# halibut

Myself and buddy Eldon

BEAUTIFUL CREATURES

Butt Munchers

Warning Warning following photo rated "R"

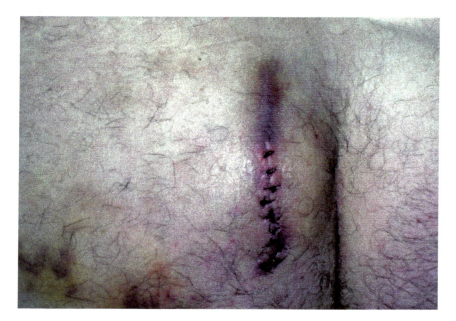

Ouch!

The Alaskan Woman

IT HAD BEEN a slow day of trolling for kings. I had four, die-hard king salmon fishermen on the boat, and I was doing everything I could think of to get a fish to bite. But to no avail. By midafternoon, I decided to make another move to a new location about eight miles down the bank, called Coney Island, a local favorite spot.

When we arrived, we joined six or seven other boats trolling the same area. Just seeing other boats in the area gave my group renewed hope. If there were this many boats in the area there must be fish, they thought. After two hours of trolling without even a bite and not seeing any action on the other boats, my boat's renewed hope had fizzled.

Not only was the fishing slow but the weather wasn't cooperating either. There was a steady drizzle and a cool southeast wind. My cold crew soon abandoned the deck and all moved into the warm cabin and turned to playing cards and telling stories. These are definitely the toughest days to be a guide. If fish aren't there, or are just taking a day off, there's not much you can do about it but just keep trying, switching flashers, new baits, change trolling speeds, different depths, and above all, keep a positive mental attitude. I call that PMA. You've got to have a Positive Mental Attitude. If you don't have PMA, you're not going to catch many fish, and you're not going to get many return customers either.

While trolling by another boat, one of my clients noticed what looked to be a woman driving the passing boat. After looking closer through the binoculars, I could confirm a young lady sitting off the stern corner of the boat, trolling for kings. Not only was she out in the elements trolling in her sixteen-foot open boat, but she also had a young child, probably about five or six years old, all geared up and eagerly sitting by his pole. This was quite a sight. This gal was a real Alaskan fisherwoman. A little wind and rain wasn't going to bother her day on the water.

About half an hour later, we were trolling alongside the smaller boat again. All of us came out of the warm cabin to take a closer look at the young lady and her little boy. One of the men on my boat asked her how the fishing was.

She smiled, "It's a slow day, but any day of fishing is a good day!"

"Holy shit!" one man whispered on my boat, "Do you see what I see?"

Under closer investigation, we realized that not only did she have a small child with her, but she had a baby, somehow strapped or harnessed to her chest! My sissy crew was all wide-eyed and amazed at what they were witnessing. I continued trolling down the bank alongside the gal and her children. This was definitely the highlight of the charter so far.

Almost as if it was scripted, one of the lady's rods slapped down toward the water. She had a king on! She jumped up, somehow unfastened her baby and set it into a basket of some sort, grabbed the rod, and began fighting the fish. This gal was really good.

The fish made a couple runs, and then she slowly worked him to the boat. The little guy sat the whole time and watched his mom in action. Soon the young lady reached for the net. She guided the salmon right into the net, set her pole down, and lifted aboard a thirty-pound king. She gave her little boy a big hug.

My boat was ecstatic. We were all yelling congrats. One of my clients hollered, "We're looking for a fishing guide tomorrow. How's your schedule?" Ouch, that hurt. We had all witnessed a real, true Alaskan lady! The gal then grabbed her little baby and reharnessed the little bundle back on her chest. She gave us a big smile and a wave and headed for town.

THE ALASKAN WOMAN

The guys just looked in disbelief, "Where is she going? Why would she quit now?"

I smiled and said, "Well, if she's going to have dinner prepared by six o'clock, it's time for her to go!"

We never did catch our fish that day, but just watching the true Alaskan lady in action had made the day.

Ka-Sploosh

IT WAS 5:00 a.m. and the *Julie Kay* was just idling out of the harbor to go king salmon fishing. This morning I had Dennis, Dwayne, Bruce, and a new client, Dave, also known as The Silver Fox onboard. Dave was in his fifties and had the whitest of whitest hair, and not one out of place. He also liked his cologne. To put it short, Dave always smelled and looked good for the fishing trips.

Just as I was about to put the throttles to the *Julie Kay* and get her on step, Dave yelled out, "I forgot my camera!" I backed off the throttle and told Dave I could just idle into the nearby dock, and he could go up the hill to his hotel and get his camera.

Dave insisted, "No, no. It's my mistake so let's just go fishing." Dennis and the rest of the group talked Dave into going after his camera. It was a beautiful day, and there was a good chance we might see whales, porpoises, eagles, and even black bears on the beaches. It would just take ten minutes to get his camera.

I was idling toward the dock when I heard a *bang-ka-sploosh* and then a "Man overboard!" Dave had jumped for the dock. The only problem was that I wasn't even close to the dock yet. I ran to the deck just in time to see Dave shooting up out of the water. He looked like one of those penguins in Antarctica shooting out of the water and up onto land. Dennis, Dwayne, and Bruce all grabbed him as he shot up like a missile out of the water and brought him back aboard. He looked like a cold, drowned rat.

I circled around again to park the boat, and Dave let me get all

KA-SPLOOSH

the way to the dock this time. After securing the boat to the dock, I told Dave to take his time, get a hot shower, and grab his camera. Dave proceeded to jump out of the boat onto the dock. He took off on a sprint up the hill to the hotel. Dave was back within eight minutes. It had to be a new record up and down that hill. He had his camera and a new set of clothes on. Dave had skipped the shower but had managed to lather on a fresh layer of cologne and comb his hair back to its perfect form again. The Silver Fox was a bit cold, but he was looking good and ready to go fishing!

While Dave was gone, his buddies had taken a board and made a walkway from the dock onto the boat. They were snickering, but Dave didn't see the humor in this. They all got on the boat, but Dave was still on the dock.

"Dan," Dave said, "I'll untie the stern line for you." Dave was always very helpful. I told him I could get it, but he insisted. So he did. He bent over to untie the line, and I heard a little *sploosh*. Dave's two-hundred-dollar French Vuarnet sunglasses had fallen off his head and into the water. He was on his belly, armpit deep, trying to grab them as they slowly slipped out of sight. He then finished untying the stern line. There were smiles on everyone's face, but no one spoke. Dave got on the boat still shaking from his earlier sea bath. "It's going to be one of those days!"

It was a tough start. It was only 5:30 a.m., and Dave had already done his morning water aerobics and had lost his expensive sunglasses. Everyone was on board, and we were off to the fishing grounds. Dennis and the guys had me chartered for four days. Today, we were headed for Frederick Point to fish for kings. It was early June, and the king run had been pretty steady.

We arrived at Frederick Point within thirty minutes and began getting the lines in the water. It is always a special treat to have Dennis and his buddies on the boat. They like to do everything themselves, so I basically just drive the boat. I gave them a demonstration of how to bait the hooks and how to deploy the electric downriggers, and then just got out of the way. Dennis is a very good fisherman, and it doesn't take him long to master the downriggers and my baiting technique.

We were trolling four rods—two rods stacked on each downrigger. The biggest problem the boys were having was trying to get the gear in the water too fast. I told them to take their time and make sure the herring were rolling and the flashers were dodging back and forth. Being in a big hurry, and putting your gear down too quickly, can add up to a big, ugly, tangled mess.

Another common, but expensive mistake is known as "the losing of the downrigger ball." When deploying the fourteen-pound lead downrigger ball to a desired depth, it must be dropped at a medium-steady speed. If the operator backs the clutch off the downrigger too fast, the ball will free fall at an out-of-control speed. Usually the operator panics and tries to stop the ball all at once by quickly tightening up on the clutch. The cable stops deploying, but the downrigger ball continues to plunge to the bottom, where it remains forever.

Another way the downrigger ball is lost, is when retrieving the ball. Just a flip of a switch and the ball automatically retrieves. The downrigger is set so that it should automatically shut off at the water's surface. Like I said, it *should* stop, but when you have multiple fishermen operating the downriggers, this auto shut-off feature doesn't always stop the ball. If the operator is not paying attention and doesn't hit the stop switch when the ball clears the surface, the ball will ascend into the aluminum downrigger arm. *Bang* and *ka sploosh*, "the losing of the downrigger ball."

At thirty dollars a ball, these mistakes can get very expensive very quickly. Dennis and the guys had used my downriggers before, and they always boarded the boat with an extra five downrigger balls. They knew I didn't carry enough spares to keep up with their losses. I would give helpful hints and guidance, but basically, I was the driver and the cameraman.

I would take their cameras and film and take pictures when they hooked a fish. They lost their share of fish, but they were doing it all on their own. I had to keep reminding myself that this is a job. Fishing with this crew is too much fun to be a job! I climbed on top of the boat to film Dave bringing in about a thirty-five-pound king. He fought it for a while and soon got it close to the boat. I got the big king zoomed into the video camera as he swam near the boat.

The next thing I saw was the net behind the fish. Bruce was attempting to net Dave's big king tail first. He had the fish about a quarter of the way in, and the salmon bolted out of the net. The fish was still hooked, and Bruce got away with a big mistake. Always net the nose first. Never, ever try to net a fish tail first. The king will feel the net coming from behind him and bolt, and there's a good chance he will get off. Dave maneuvered the king close again, and this time the camcorder showed a big king coming into view, and then a net appeared and swooped around the fish nose first. Bruce successfully netted Dave's big king!

Now it was time to get the lines back in the water. I was letting them fly solo this time. Dave and Dennis were working one downrigger, and Dwayne and Bruce were managing the other. I was barely able to get the boat in gear and trolling again before baits and flashers were being launched over the side. Bruce and Dwayne had managed to get both rods stacked on one downrigger and they were fishing.

Dave and Dennis were working on getting a new bait on Dave's line. It wasn't the prettiest herring I'd ever seen, but it definitely looked like a wounded baitfish—a severely wounded baitfish with no scales. Now they were ready to stack the lines on the downrigger. Dave let his line out twenty feet behind the boat. The flasher was wobbling, and the bait was darting side to side. It actually looked good. He hooked his line into the release clip and loosened his drag on the reel. Dennis backed off the clutch on the downrigger, and down the first line went. Dennis tightened the clutch to stop the ball from descending. Now Dennis dropped his bait back about twenty feet to take a look. It looked great! He clipped his line into the second release, loosened his drag, backed the clutch off the downrigger, and both lines began to drop. Dennis was watching the line counter on the downrigger, and as it hit eighty feet, he went to tighten the downrigger drag. But he turned it the wrong way. The downrigger ball picked up to out-of-control speed. Dennis realized what was happening, but it was too late. When he tried to put the brakes on the ball, it just continued to the bottom. One more downrigger ball had escaped. Eighty feet was the plan; four hundred feet straight to the bottom became the ball's final destination.

Dennis and Dave's side would need some rerigging before they would be fishing again. I looked at the other two rods, and something looked awry. The poles were making strange movements, definitely not the kind of movements caused by a fish on the other end. "Well guys, I hate to say this, but I think you need to bring your lines up and make sure your gear is working."

They looked at me like I was crazy. "We just got our lines in and now you want us to take them out?" Bruce and Dwayne began retrieving the lines. When Dwayne's came up to the surface, so did Bruce's, all together in one big clump. In the excitement, they had been in such a hurry to get everything back in the water. So the gear went down in a tangle and came up in a glob of flashers and bait. We now had four rods on board and none in the water.

"Okay," I said, "No big deal. Let's just slow everything down a bit, and we'll get the rods back in the water, one at a time. The only way to get better is to screw up and keep learning from your mistakes."

KA-SPLOOSH

The guys got better and better at using the downriggers as the day went on. By the end of the day, they had all caught kings, and lost a few too. It had been a great day. It was about 5:00 p.m. and I said, "Let's call it a day and we'll hit it early again tomorrow."

The rods were all out of the water. The final downrigger ball was ascending to the surface. Dennis looked at me and said, "Can you believe it, Dan? We only lost three downrigger balls today. That must be a record." I pointed at his downrigger as the ball came smashing into the metal arm. *Ka-bam*, and *ka-sploosh*. Dennis just looked at me, "Four still isn't that bad!" To town we went. We needed to take care of fish and replenish our downrigger ball stock for tomorrow.

Coffee Anyone?

THIS MORNING BROUGHT rain and wind. Everyone donned full rain gear and warmer clothes. It wasn't a bad day, if you were dressed for it. The Silver Fox had the newest of new rain gear, all color coordinated. He looked good and smelled even better. Dave was soon untying the boat from the dock. This day, we were going after salmon again, but before we headed out, herring jigging was on the agenda.

I would idle the boat in front of the harbor looking for a ball of herring on the sounder (fish finder). When I'd see herring, I'd stop and have the guys drop their herring jigs into the water. A jig consists of five or six small hooks. The herring feed on krill (small crustaceans) and mistake the hooks for a meal. Four, five, even six herring at a time started coming aboard. It didn't take long before we had a bucket of fresh, wiggling herring. You can't beat a fresh herring for king salmon bait.

Today we decided to try our luck at Beacon Point, just a thirty-minute run from town. The guys were in scramble mode getting hooks baited and lines in the water. They had become familiar with the downriggers, and getting the gear in the water with a good presentation was becoming routine. Losing a cannon ball here and there was also routine.

It was definitely a coffee morning. Everyone was drinking coffee, watching the rods, and waiting for the first rod to spring off a downrigger. Dennis walked out back and took a leak. He had an interesting method of peeing over the side. He took a leak in a Styrofoam cup and then poured it over the side. This way he got no pee on the side of the boat. That can often happen using the conventional peeing-straight-into-the-water method. Just when you've got your hands busy doing one thing, that's when a fish hits.

Soon enough, the back corner rod took a dive and our first king was hooked. Within seconds, the cabin was empty and the deck was full of fishermen. Dave was playing the fish and Dennis, Dwayne, and Bruce were quickly getting the other rods and downriggers out of the way. I would just stay out of the way and watch the show. Dave soon had the fish alongside the boat. This was a nice king and had a lot of fight left. We all watched the king shake his head side to side just out of reach of the net. This is a helpless feeling, when there's not a thing you can do but hope the line doesn't get sawed off by the razor-sharp teeth of a big king.

Dave's rod took an abrupt snap back, and the king slowly disappeared with Dave's broken leader still in his mouth. Dave had done everything right; sometimes it just doesn't matter. That's why they call it fishing and not "let's go catching."

Soon the gear was back in the water and everyone was huddled in the cabin drinking newly poured hot coffee. It was a cold, rainy day, and hot coffee helped take the chill off. While we drank, Dennis headed back to the deck to relieve himself again. A call came from the back deck, "Has anyone seen my Styrofoam pee cup?" In the excitement of the fish, Dennis had misplaced his pee cup. All coffee drinking came to an abrupt halt! A pee cup was missing in action, and there was a good chance one of us had a Styrofoam cup of coffee with a little extra wang in it.

Dennis chuckled, "It's no big deal guys, I shook it out when I was done!" We never did figure out who was drinking from the pee cup that day, but from then on, everyone put their name on their Styrofoam cup when they got on the boat.

We continued to troll but to no avail. The guys kept working the gear—changing flashers and baits—but the fish didn't seem interested (or they just weren't there). The weather had kicked up, and it was raining sideways. No fish and ugly weather makes for a long day on the water.

We pulled up the gear and changed locations, thinking maybe the fish had moved to another spot about six miles down the shore. After two more hours of nothing, it was time to make another move. This was going to be one of those long days. We were determined to catch just one fish. There's nothing worse than freezing your butt off all day and coming back to town empty-handed...skunked.

It was six o'clock and everyone was wet, cold, and tired. Except Dave. He was just wet and cold. Dave would fish twenty-four hours a day if he could. I think he even fishes in his sleep.

Just when I was going to wave the white surrender flag and call it a day, Dwayne's rod took off. Dave was the first one out of the cabin. Next, Bruce, Dennis, and then Dwayne came stumbling out. The rocking and rolling boat was a challenge and would make landing a king that much tougher. As the guys were clearing the rods, I was taking baits off lines and putting the poles away for the ride home. Dwayne was either going to be a hero or a zero. Everyone gave him plenty of encouragement and helpful hints. "Take your time, let him run, don't horse him, and don't blow it, Dwayne. This is the last chance!" All the pressure was on Dwayne. It was a big, beautiful, bright silver king salmon. Dwayne asked if I would net his fish.

"I thought you'd never ask," I replied. I think I wanted this fish in the boat as much as he did. Dwayne played his fish to perfection. Finally, one last run and up the side of the boat and into the net he came. We were not skunked! Patience and persistence had paid off. Dwayne had just landed a beautiful thirty-five-pound king.

Dave looked up at the rods all put away. He looked at me half-dazed. "The bite's on, Dan, we need to get these poles back in the water!" He continued pleading, "It's going to be a late-evening bite. We can't quit now!"

Sorry, Dave, there would be no late-evening bites. The F/V *Julie Kay* was heading home. It was a bouncy ride back to the harbor, and everyone except Dave was spent—5:00 a.m. to 8:00 p.m. for one fish. I slipped the boat into the stall, and Dave jumped out and began securing the bowline. Before I could even get out of the boat, our savior, Dwayne, headed to the cleaning table with his nice fish. He was beaming with satisfaction. He had saved the day! I secured the stern line.

Before the rest of the guys even got off the boat, Dwayne had returned to the boat. He was as white as a ghost and shaking. If I didn't know any better, I'd say he was in shock. He was looking at us, but saying nothing. Dennis knew exactly what had happened and said, "You didn't!"

Dwayne just nodded his head up and down. He had tossed his fish on the cleaning table, and it had slipped right off the end of the table and into the water. Dwayne was able to grab its tail, but the fish was too heavy and slippery. Dwayne could not hang on. The fish was gone and would soon be dinner for a local sea lion. Poor, poor Dwayne. He had gone from hero to a zero in just a few seconds. He had come up with a new method of catch and release. It had been a long day with a sad, sad ending.

Halibut Don't Fight

AFTER THE PREVIOUS long, cold day of slow king salmon action, the guys voted to go halibut fishing. This was Dave's first time at "butt" fishing. Dennis kept us entertained with a couple of funny stories on the way to the halibut grounds. Before we knew it, I was anchoring the boat on a pinnacle where I'd been having good success earlier in the week. The weather was still cool, but the winds and the seas had calmed since yesterday. The nice thing about halibut fishing is all the action. There's always something on the bottom that's hungry. Bullheads, cod, rockfish, turbot, halibut, and even an octopus may grab a baited hook at any time.

The anchor was set. It was almost time to drop the lines. We were fishing in two hundred feet of water. Each pole was rigged with an eighty-pound test for the main line. The main line was connected to a spreader bar (stainless steel device used to keep the bait from tangling with the weight and main line), and off the spreader bar was a five-hundred-pound test leader with a giant circle hook at the end. We were using two pounds of lead on the short end of the spreader bar to get the lines to the bottom. Each rig was baited with fresh herring. The anchor was set, the rods were rigged, and it was time to drop our tasty offerings to the bottom.

The Silver Fox was wound tighter than a coiled spring. He was ready to catch his first halibut! The guys had been feeding him stories of past successful halibut trips, and he was shaking with excitement.

The lines had only been on the bottom five minutes, and Dave was growing impatient. I reassured him that it was normal not to get bites immediately. The bait scent takes time to move around the area. I told him that if we didn't start getting action within an hour, we would try a different location. But we needed to give this spot time, and let the scent move around. I assured him our first victim would come cruising along soon.

Sure enough, after about thirty minutes, the action picked up. Codfish, turbot, and small halibut were being caught. The halibut were too small to keep, but the cod were cut into chunks for halibut bait.

Dave was getting bites, but not hooking them. Up would come his line for a bait check, and down it would go reloaded with fresh cod and herring. He was growing more and more frustrated every time a fish stole a meal. "Dan, what am I doing wrong? Is my hook sharp? Do I have too much bait on? Is my line too far off the bottom?"

I told Dave, "Patience, just relax. Just let the fish hook himself. If you start getting a bite, just hold steady, don't jerk. Let the fish hook himself. Just do the opposite of salmon fishing. Don't set the hook." Not setting the hook is the secret to catching fish on a circle hook.

Dave nodded his head. "Okay, I'll try to have patience." Patience is one thing Dave does not possess, and he's the first one to admit it. Dave wanted to catch a fish…now!

He took my advice, and lo and behold, Dave got a small halibut on. Dave cranked down his drag and brought the small fish in at record speed. "These fish don't even fight," he remarked.

I explained to Dave that a small fish was no match for the heavy gear we were using. I assured him a large fish would give him a real challenge. Dave didn't believe me. He had it set in his mind that a halibut was just a flat, lazy, non-fighting fish. Dave had no idea just how powerful a big halibut was, but he was about to find out.

Dave's pole took a slow, steady bend, and kept bending. I could tell it was a big fish by the way it took the bait. The smaller fish peck away at the bait and then drop it and continue to peck at the bait until it's gone or they get hooked. The big guys just suck the bait in and start to swim away with it. When the line comes tight, the circle hook twists into the corner of their mouth and the fish is hooked.

Dave grabbed his bending rod. He was going to show us how easy it was to bring in a lazy, non-fighting halibut! The 145-pound Silver Fox was in for a real eye opener. Dave had been cranking in small fish with full drag. He had not loosened his drag before the big fish hit. Dave was going to go power against power, mano y mano with the fish. Dave looked like he was in a boxing match. His silver hair whipped up, down, up, down, up, down. The fish was just giving Dave a few little head shakes. I told Dave, "You might want to loosen up the drag."

Dave, a little punch drunk insisted, "These things don't fight!" The halibut realized he was hooked and began swimming away. Dave's rod bent double, and he was forced to stagger to the side of the boat. The pull on the rod was too much, and Dave was dragged to the rail like a rag doll. The rod was pinned on the rail, and Dave was hanging on for dear life. He was at the point of no return.

It was evident that Dave was not going to loosen the drag. With the stretch gone out of the line, the moment of truth had arrived. Would Dave get dragged into the water? Would Dave let go of the rod? Would the line break? One thing for sure…the outcome would not favor Dave.

Dave's rod suddenly lost all bend. Dave had so much pressure on the rod, he almost landed on his back when his line snapped. Dave didn't even make it through the first round and had been knocked out by a lazy, slow-moving halibut. The Silver Fox, with his hair a mess, looked like a deer in headlights. "What the hell was that? Do you have sharks in these waters? I know that was not a halibut." He continued with a dazed look, "Dennis, halibut don't fight."

We were all in tears after watching Dave get his ass kicked by a fish. Thank God, the line broke. I know Dave well and he would have gone in the water again before he let go of the rod. To this day, The Silver Fox is still convinced that he had something besides a halibut on the end of his line.

HALIBUT DON'T FIGHT

Very Bottom

THE NEXT MORNING found us right back where we had finished fishing the day before. The guys wanted action, and halibut fishing was the perfect match. On this day, we were getting plenty of action and catching lots of halibut, but nothing of any size. I had everyone start using bigger baits, and soon the fish were getting larger. Bruce was really having a good day. Every time he dropped his bait to the bottom, he got a fish. Everyone soon had a limit of halibut. No big fish today, but lots of nice halibut in the thirty- to fifty-pound range.

Dave landed a couple, but he was still dreaming about the one that had taken him to the rail. He was still not convinced it was really a halibut. On the way back to town, Bruce enlightened us with his secret of why he was catching most of the fish. "It's simple," he began, "a nice-sized chunk of codfish tipped with a piece of herring. Then I drop my line to the bottom, and then I continue to let more line out 'til I get to the very, very bottom. Let her sit a couple minutes and *bam!* Fish on every time."

We all just listened, thinking the same thing. Finally, Dwayne asked Bruce what the difference between the bottom and the very, very bottom was.

"It's simple," Bruce replied. "You guys are just letting your lines to the bottom and stopping right there. I'm hitting the bottom and then I continue letting line out until I hit the very, very bottom." Bruce looked at us like we were a bunch of idiots. He was convinced there were two bottoms: the main bottom and the "very, very bottom."

Dennis finally spoke up, "Bruce, we are all dropping our lines down to the same damn bottom…the only bottom."

Bruce just smiled and said, "Well, evidently we were fishing on different bottoms because I was the one catching all the fish, and I was on the very, very bottom." I just listened and thought that there must have been a few fish on the other bottom because everyone caught fish.

I told Bruce he would have to sign an agreement that he would never come to Petersburg to start a guiding business. With his fishing theories, he might put me and the other guides out of business!

Hard Luck and the Silver Fox

IT WAS THE last day of the four-day charter, and the guys wanted to go after halibut one more time. Dave wanted another chance at the big one that got away. Dave is an avid mountain climber. He has conquered many famous mountains, and now his sights were on a big, big halibut.

This morning began as a very cool day with a slight breeze. Dave is very cold-blooded, and he was really dressed to the hilt. Layer upon layer of clothing went under his stylish rain gear. Dave also wore some sort of heavy gloves. They were not the regular rubber gloves but more like gloves you would wear to demolish a house. They were thick gloves, and the outside of them was made of a sandpaper material. Dave was dressed warmly, except for his head—no hat, didn't want to mess up the perfect hair. The Silver Fox had gone over the battle plan. He would be patient and let the fish get hooked and swore he would not mess with the already-set drag. Power against power with a really big fish never ends well.

Bruce was off and running with a nice forty-pound halibut. The very, very bottom was producing for him again. Soon, Dennis and Dwayne followed with nice halibut. Dave was catching cod and small halibut. Up to the surface, down to the bottom, up down, up down, Dave would go as fast as he could reel. He was trying to give himself as much fishing time on the bottom as possible. The more time on the bottom, the more chances for his quarry.

Dwayne had been dubbed with a new nickname, "Hard Luck,"

after losing a really big king earlier in the trip and then catching a beautiful king just to see it slide off the cleaning table. The new nickname suited him perfectly. Hard Luck is one of the nicest, down-to-earth guys I have ever met. He does have a bit of a black cloud over him when it comes to fishing though. Every time he gets a really nice fish on, he always looks over at me with a "something bad is going to happen" look. And something usually goes wrong. Today would be no different!

Dwayne was hooked up with a really big fish. His line was screaming off the reel. Dennis and Dave quickly retrieved their lines and brought them in the boat to prevent a tangle with Dwayne's fish.

Bruce was delaying his retrieval because he was getting a bite. To get to the very, very bottom, Bruce had a significant amount of extra line out. A minute later, and Bruce was pumping and reeling. He had hooked a fish too.

Bruce was claiming he had a big one on also. Something wasn't right. Every time Dwayne's fish would take line, so would Bruce's. The two anglers were definitely tangled. Bruce insisted he had a big one on also, but the rest of the boat wasn't so sure, especially Hard Luck. A dark cloud had appeared. Dwayne gave me his, "something bad is going to happen" look.

What should have happened was for Bruce to loosen on his drag, so when Dwayne's fish went on a run there would be no extra tension or fraying on the lines. That's what *should* have happened. But that is not what actually happened. Dwayne was slowly bringing his fish up, and, amazingly enough, Bruce's fish was also coming up at the same time! Then Dwayne's halibut made a final run to the bottom. A final run!

There was too much tension between the two lines, and Hard Luck's rod went limp. Once again, the fish gods were not on Dwayne's side. He didn't even look back at me this time. Dwayne retrieved his remaining empty line and put his rod in the holder.

Meanwhile, Bruce was still working on a fish. Then from the depth, Bruce's trophy came into view. It was a five-pound "ping pong paddle" (baby halibut). Bruce was right. He did have a fish on! Dwayne just shook his head wondering what he'd done wrong to be blessed with such bad luck.

The day continued with lots of action but no big fish. The Silver Fox was growing impatient. He was tired of reeling in and releasing small fish; he wanted a big one as soon as possible.

Dave asked me what I would do if I wanted to catch a big halibut. The answer was easy: big, big bait. Whack the whole tail off the cod and then slide the circle hook through the meat and skin of the bait. You won't get many bites on a bait of this size. The smaller fish will try to suck it in but will lose interest. When a big girl comes by, she will suck the whole bait in. They don't get big by being picky eaters. When a big fish grabs the bait, you must have patience and give the victim ample time to hook itself. The bigger the bait, the tougher it is to hook a fish. Dave was ready to use my *big bait, big fish* theory, and he was going to do his best to be patient!

Dave dropped his big cod tail to the bottom and began testing his patience. Dennis, Bruce, and Dwayne were busy catching fish. Dave was busy pacing back and forth and looking at his limp rod—no bites, not even a hint of a bite. Then, he would reel his tail all the way to the surface to make sure it was still on. Not even David Copperfield could get that bait off without making his rod bounce. Dave just looked at the big tail and reluctantly sent it back to the bottom. Having his buddies catching fish all around him was testing what little patience he had.

Five minutes would go by and Dave would ask, "Dan, do you think I should check my bait?" I would reassure him that there was no need to check and that I was sure he still had bait on. Nothing was going to get that tail off without him knowing it.

Dave was just about to give up on the big bait theory when his rod took a big bend and the line slowly started slipping off the reel. A big fish had hold of the tail and was slowly swimming away with it. I told Dave to just leave the rod alone until the fish really starts peeling the line off. That's when you know he is hooked.

HARD LUCK AND THE SILVER FOX

The Silver Fox was a tightly coiled spring. The line began smoking off the reel. Dave was hooked up with another big halibut. Dave grabbed his rod, and all of the other rods were brought to the surface. I told Dave his drag was set at a safe setting. He reassured me that he would not mess with the drag.

The fish continued on a long run, and Dave was concerned he was going to run out of line. Finally, the halibut slowed down, and Dave was slowly getting line back. Thirty minutes later, the halibut was straight below the boat, and Dave had him slowly coming up off the bottom. He gained a little line each time the rod was lifted up… lift up, reel down, lift up, reel down. As long as Dave lifted slowly on the pole, the drag was not slipping. The Silver Fox was gaining on the big bruiser. Dave just needed to stay the course, and he was going to land his big halibut.

While Dave worked the fish, I got out the shark hook and tied it to three hundred feet of heavy line and then secured the end to a cleat. I explained to Dave what the plan was. "When the fish comes up, I will slip the shark hook into the roof of its mouth. Then we will have her on your line and also on the big line. The fish will most likely make a final run, and we will let her. Then I'll slowly retrieve the line with the shark hook, and you will retrieve your line at the same time. When the halibut comes up again, I will hit her right between the eyes with my size 34 aluminum bat and then tie her off to the side of the boat, and we'll have her."

Dave just nodded his head. He was an absolute nervous wreck. He was literally shaking, and his hair was a mess. He was so close to the top of the mountain. This non-fighting, slow-moving fish had become a real challenge for Dave, and the completion of his quest was near. I again went over the final game plan with Dave and told him one more time, "If the fish wants to run, don't mess with the drag!"

No sooner did I say, "Let her run," than the big brute headed for the bottom one last time. Dave saw the line disappearing off his reel. Let her run, don't mess with the drag, be patient, relax. Brain overloaded, too much information, short circuit…it was as if it were in

DROPPING MY LINES

slow motion!

Dave's sandpaper demolition glove slowly covered the reel. He pressed his thumb on the line as it was smoking off the reel. You could smell and see the sandpapery rubber material flying in the air as it sawed through the line. It was too late. The line snapped right at the reel—actually right at Dave's sandpaper thumb! The Silver Fox was a mess. All he could say was, "I didn't mess with the drag." The smell of burning rubber was still in the air. The mountain climber was not going to make it to the summit today.

This was the last day of the charter, but there would be many more in the years ahead. Dennis, his family, and friends have been fishing with me for thirty years and continue to come back year after year. I look forward to their return every June. These are the kind of people that make my job so much fun. They are great friends.

My great friend Dennis and myself with a beauty

Warning!

IT WAS ANOTHER typically beautiful day in Petersburg. Today we were halibut fishing. I had two couples from Tennessee: John and Barb, and Pete and Betsy. Three out of four of the group had experience at fishing.

Betsy was not one of the three. Just getting this gal on the boat was a challenge. She was terrified of the water. Before we could get her on board, we secured a life jacket around her. Why she was going fishing was beyond me, but she was a hoot. Her husband, Pete, had warned me that you never know what she's going to say. Sometimes she just opens her mouth and surprise! It just comes out. I wasn't exactly sure what Pete meant, but I guess I'd been warned.

As the day went on, Betsy slowly began to get a bit more comfortable on the water, and started really enjoying the trip. By early afternoon, everyone had caught a nice halibut, except for Betsy. She had been busy catching everyone else's lines all day long. Betsy would reel her line up to check her bait while standing directly in the middle of the boat. In her mind, the safest place on the boat was in the middle. If she got near the side, she was afraid she would just fall over, or a sea monster might grab her and pull her in the water. Betsy's unique way of fishing was putting her line in everybody else's. Pete and I gently tried to nudge her to the side, but she was a statue and would not budge. I thought I was the "tangle master," but Betsy was putting me to the test!

Finally, after endless tangles, Betsy had something on…something other than her partners' lines. She had a halibut on! That's when the

WARNING!

show began, (the rated R show). Standing in the middle of the boat, Betsy was using every technique of reeling in a fish I'd ever seen, and some techniques I didn't think were even possible. The way she was struggling, and looking at the bend of the rod, it looked like she was fighting a good-sized fish.

Pete was trying to help his wife position the butt of the rod on her hip but wasn't having much luck. Betsy continued to pump and reel and was really working up a froth. I noticed her face had dropped closer to her reel. The more Betsy cranked, the closer her head was. The next thing we knew, her damn head was almost in her own reel. Then I saw it. The strap on Betsy's life jacket had dropped into the reel, and she had reeled her head damn near into the reel!

I thought I'd seen it all, but this was a first. Hell, Betsy had herself pinned in her own reel! "Hang on here," I said, "we need to let a bunch of line out so we can get your face out of your reel."

Soon we had her free, and Betsy was off to the races again! She was trying to reel with the rod butt under her armpit, and it wasn't working very well. Pete finally yelled, "Hun, it's no time to be a lady; just put the end of your pole in your crotch!"

Betsy took his advice, "Hey this works pretty good, and it feels good too! Wow, I'm really starting to enjoy this fishing thing more and more!" I had been warned. She just opens it up and out it comes!

We were all in tears watching Betsy trying to get this fish in. Still standing in the middle of the boat, she now had her fish, plus three other lines. This was surely going to be the tangle from hell! Betsy was pulling everyone's weights, plus her fish, and she was struggling. She was sticking to the rod-in-the-crotch method, and it seemed to be working for her.

We had almost quit laughing when her mouth opened again. "Jesus Christ! If I don't get this son of a bitch in soon, I'm going to need a new vagina!" Pete's morning warning all made sense now. I thought I'd seen it all, but I was wrong. I thought I had heard it all, but I was wrong. She actually had me turning red. Can you imagine the sound of that phrase with a strong Tennessee accent? It sounded more like "a new vaginer."

Pete apologized for his wife. I had come to the conclusion that there were two totally different women inside this gal's body: Nervous Betsy and Nasty Patsy. After a brief silence, the boat was in tears again.

Finally, up came the fish. A fifteen-pound halibut completely wrapped up in four lines, leads, hooks, and baits! Betsy looked at me, "There's no way you're letting him go because he's too small!"

She was right. Anyone who fights a fifteen pounder for an hour deserves to keep it. It was the last fish of the day, and it had been a day to remember. I had been warned!

WARNING!

Bait!

OF ALL THE sport fishing charters I've done, there's almost always a good memory to take away from each trip. People go sport fishing to have a good time. When the weather doesn't cooperate, or the fishing is just slow, a good time is usually still available. Just being on vacation and getting out on a boat with friends, catching up on old times, and sharing each other's stories can make for a special day, even when the fish and weather are not cooperating.

Like I said, *almost* all my trips end with a good memory. I believe God created a very minute percentage of people just for the purpose of being a pain in everyone's ass. I think these people leave the house in the morning with one thought. *How many people can I piss off today?* Thankfully, it's very rare that I run into these special pieces of God's work. When I do get the pleasure of taking these types out on a charter, the first thing I do when I get home is go to my calendar and write "RED FLAG" next to their name. When they call to go fishing again, I'll see they have been red-flagged and I'll say, "Sorry, I'm full" and refer them to one of my buddies. They do the same for me.

This morning, I was taking two couples halibut fishing. My seventeen-year-old daughter, Julie, was also on board today as my crew. John and Judy from Portland, Oregon, had fished with me before and were always great fun to have on the boat. The other couple, Troy and Marge, from New York, would be fishing with me for the first time.

I had a bad feeling this might be one of those charters from hell before I even left the dock. Troy's wife, Marge, called me the evening before the charter and asked if I could stop by their bed and breakfast, pick them up, and bring them to the boat. "Not a problem," I said. I told her I'd be there just before 6:00 a.m.

The next morning, I arrived ten minutes before six. I waited for a few minutes in the truck hoping they would come walking out the door, but no such luck. I knocked and Marge opened the door. She informed me that I was early and it would be about fifteen minutes before they'd be finished eating breakfast. She told me they would be out when they were done. I went back to the truck and impatiently waited, thinking to myself, *My feeling was right. This is going to be a charter from hell.*

Fifteen minutes later, the door opened and out they came. Instead of getting in the truck, Marge came to my driver's window. She spoke, "Dan, I have one more request. I have a rental car and we need to drop it off on the way to the boat. So, if you could follow us, I'll just drop it off and we will be ready to go."

I bit my lip really hard and said, "Okay." I knew Julie and the other couple were already at the boat and were probably wondering where I was.

I followed Marge and Troy to the Tides Inn where they were dropping off their car. I waited for ten minutes for them to return. Finally, I went inside to see what the holdup was. Marge was at the front counter tearing some poor gal and her manager a new ass. I could hear her yelling, "You're out of your blankety-blank minds if you think you're going to charge me that much a gallon because the car is being returned with a half tank of gas!" Marge looked at me, "Dan, you need to follow me to the fuel station so I can fill the car up, and then we'll drop it off. If they think I'm going to pay two dollars over the normal price for gas, they're out of their minds!"

I am a very easy-going, patient man, but Marge had broken me. "Okay," I said, "but just so you know, you are on the clock; your charter has started. It's not going to matter what time we leave the dock; the boat will be back at 3:30 p.m. or sooner." I was really hoping Marge would fire me, but I wasn't to be so lucky. She opted to pay the extra fifteen dollars for the gas, and she and Troy headed back for the truck.

I smiled at the two behind the counter and told them I had two extra seats on the boat if they wanted to join us for the day. "You couldn't pay us enough money to go on your boat!" the gal boasted. I was right; Marge and her husband had only been out of bed for about an hour and a half, and they had already managed to make enemies with each person they had come into contact with.

Ten minutes later, I finally got Marge and Troy to the boat. The two couples and Julie exchanged pleasantries, and the *Julie Kay* was finally underway. On our way to the fishing grounds, Julie, Judy, John, and I received a seminar on sail boating skills and all about the years and years of fishing experience Marge and Troy had. We got to listen to the experienced yachtsman and the professional fisherman for the longest hour and twenty minutes of my life. They continued on and then began to question me about my daughter's experience level and ability to be my crew.

Finally, we were to the fishing grounds. I dropped the anchor, and Julie rigged and baited everyone's rods. The plan was to fish one couple off the stern corners and the other couple off the port and starboard sides. This was normally the way I fished. The cabin blocks the wind, and the poles can be quickly rebaited without going back and forth to the bow. The fish could be landed much easier from the back deck of the boat, and everyone gets to enjoy each other's company.

Today was not a normal day. The professionals insisted that they wanted to fish off the bow. It actually didn't sound like such a bad idea, as it seemed everyone had already enjoyed about as much of their company as they could take. Soon Troy and his lovely wife were fishing off the bow. John and Judy had the back deck all to themselves. It was great to catch up on each other's lives since the last time our paths had crossed.

After about twenty minutes of fishing, but no catching, the grumbling began off the bow. Troy informed me that it looked like we were fishing in a "dry halibut hole" and it may be a smart move to change locations. I told him to have a little patience. He also informed me that he had "properly secured the bowline, since it was not done correctly by the crew."

Marge spouted, "Do you have any other kind of bait? Maybe they don't like our herring and salmon."

"The bait is fine. If we don't start getting some action in thirty minutes, we'll try another spot."

This was not the answer the professional anglers wanted to hear. "Sounds like thirty minutes of wasted time," echoed off the bow.

It seemed like an hour, but only five minutes later, John's rod went down, and soon he had a nice forty-pound halibut to the surface. John was all smiles. I knocked the fish between the eyes with my bat, and into the box he went.

Soon Judy was hooked up with a halibut too. She was having a ball getting jerked around by this fish. Ten minutes later, Judy landed her halibut. It looked to be a twin to John's, but I assured her it was bigger. John and Judy were giving hugs and high fives. They were having a great day.

I watched Troy and Marge's fishing techniques from the back of the boat. They were continuously jerking their rods up and down. The poor fish were probably getting sore necks watching their bait snap up and down, up and down. It was a lot easier to just swim over and grab John and Judy's baits that were just dangling there ten feet away.

The action had definitely picked up on the stern of the boat. John and Judy were getting steady action. The bow rods were also active but not from the fish; it was from the jerk-and-snap method.

I'd come to the conclusion that the sour pusses fishing off the bow were fishing with no bait. All their jerking and yanking had most likely jerked their baits off long ago. It's hard to give someone advice when they already know everything, but I attempted it. I went to the bow and very nicely told them that they might want to reel up and check their baits. Troy assured me that nothing had touched their baits. I patiently told Troy the method they were using might have left their hooks bare, and if it were me, I would check the bait.

Reluctantly, they began reeling in their lines.

I went back to the happy end of the boat and helped Julie bait, and release John and Judy's smaller fish. They were having a day to remember, and so was I! I looked to the bow and watched two empty, baitless hooks come to the surface. Surprise, surprise…I was actually right. The two experts looked at each other, and then came the most obnoxious sound from the bow. "BAIT! We need BAIT!" yelled Marge. Julie brought new bait for the pair and got them rebaited.

Back down to the bottom their hooks went. They instantly began getting bites, but would not give the fish a chance to eat the bait. They would wildly jerk the rod as hard as they could, trying to set the hook. "I don't like these stupid hooks," Troy muttered. Again, and again they would come up to the surface with empty hooks. "BAIT!" "Stupid hooks," and "BAIT!" echoed from the bow. Julie was earning her money today! She continued bringing new baits to the bow and catering to the "snaggletooth" and her mate.

Again, I went to the bow to offer a suggestion. It was obvious that the fishermen in the back were doing things differently than the fishermen up front. Judy and John had their limits and were now catching and releasing. Troy and his lovely wife had not caught a single fish. "Instead of continuously jigging and jerking the rod when you feel something, try letting the bait sit idle for a few minutes and then slowly jig it and then let it sit again. When you feel a bite, don't jerk, just slowly start reeling up. This works well with a circle hook. If that doesn't work for you, just drop the bait on the bottom, put your rod in the holder, and let the fish hook itself. That's the technique that's working in the back." The duo didn't like taking suggestions, but it was obvious their technique was not going to work.

I headed back to the fun end of the boat, hoping Troy and Marge would try one of my methods. I really did want them to catch a fish, but if it didn't happen, I wasn't going to lose any sleep over it!

Fishing remained steady in the back, but things didn't get any better up front. Either I was a terrible teacher, or Marge and angler Troy were lousy students! They could see how well John and Judy were doing. I think they just wanted to prove that their herky-jerky technique worked. That annoying, fingernails-on-the-chalkboard, screech from Marge became too much to bear. "BAIT, we're out of BAIT, Julie!" My poor daughter had become their little servant girl.

Julie came over to me and said, "Dad, I give up. I can't do it anymore! You need to deal with them." They had tested my patience over and over, and finally my patience valve broke. The next time Snaggletooth chanted, "BAIT, more BAIT!" I walked up to the bow and plopped a bucket of herring and salmon bellies between them.

I very nicely said, "Here's your damn bait. If you want to fish off the bow, you can bait your own hooks; I'm sure you know how. We're not going to run back and forth baiting your hooks all day." Those were not my exact words—I may have left a few choice words out. I was fed up, and it was obvious there was no winning formula for these two. I pray to God they did not breed and produce children.

With almost an hour to go on the charter, Troy finally hooked a fish. When he jerked his rod up, he hit something solid and it began taking line. "You've got a good one!" I yelled, "Let him run!"

That's not what he did. Troy continued to set the hook while the fish was running. The fish continued running without Troy's hook in it. Troy had literally jerked the fish off his hook. "That was no halibut!" he yelled, "I had hold of a shark!" Troy knew his fish; he was good.

I gave the fifteen-minute warning and then we'd be heading in. "But we haven't caught a fish!" Marge barked.

I said, "Put a fresh piece of bait on, let it to the bottom, put your pole in the holder, and don't touch it until I tell you to, and I bet you'll have a fish in five minutes." I had challenged Snaggletooth.

She actually did as I asked, and in about two minutes a halibut hooked himself. Now she just had to reel him in. Five minutes later, Marge had a twenty-pound halibut in the boat. Troy hooked one too. This time, he didn't try to break the fish's neck by jerking on it. It was another twenty pounder. In the fish box he went, and it was time to go home.

It had been a long, painful day. It was a quiet ride back to town. John and Judy were worn out from catching fish all day. Troy and Marge were not very talkative on the way back. I don't think they liked me. The feeling was mutual. When we arrived at the dock, I gave the couple options of what to do with their catch. I could fillet their fish and put it in a bag for them, or the local packing outfit could come to the boat and pick up their fish and fillet it, vacuum pack it, freeze it, box it, and get it to the airport without them even having to touch it.

John and Judy didn't mind spending a few extra dollars to have their catch taken care of right. Marge and Troy of course, didn't want to spend any money on taking care of their fish. They said they had already spent way too much on a damn charter. (Ouch, that hurt!) Troy suggested I fillet, cut pieces, individually bag in Ziplocs, and box it.

That was not one of the options. I nicely told him that that wasn't going to happen, and that they needed to go through the packing outfitter, or deal with the fish themselves. My patience button had blown again.

Doug from Coastal Cold Storage came down to the boat to get the fish. I gave John and Judy a hug before they headed up the dock. Marge and Troy were still giving the poor guy picking up the fish an ear full. "This is going to cost us how much? How do we even know we are going to get our own fish back? This is outrageous!"

Doug just bit his lip. "Just stop by the shop in the morning, and we'll have your bill ready." He quickly grabbed the cart of fish and wheeled them up the dock, shaking his head.

Marge and Troy had managed to piss another person off. Marge told me they needed a ride home. I nicely said I was going to scrub my boat, and then get fuel, and then I would gladly give them a ride home. What I really wanted to say was, "No way! This charter is over!" The happy couple headed up the ramp and headed home. We got a nice tip and some good memories from one couple, and the other couple just gave us a big pain in the ass! Red Flag…Red Flag! Some names may have been changed to protect the innocent.

Prankster

THERE IS NOTHING better than pulling off a good prank. Dad loved pulling pranks on his old buddies. Dad moved to Palm Springs about twenty-five years ago, but he usually comes back for a visit once or twice a year.

A couple of years ago, Dad came up to fish the annual salmon derby. The morning before the derby, he was going to go to the coffee shop and see if he could prank some of his old buddies who had no idea he was in town.

The morning of Dad's prank started out with some good entertainment. Cheryl and I were having coffee at about 5:30 a.m. Dad was still in bed, which was not like him. Normally he is an early riser. I'm sure that extra glass of wine before bed may have had something to do with it.

Ten minutes later, the bedroom door opened and Dad came stumbling down the hallway. He plopped down on the couch still half-asleep. He put one sock on, and then was having problems getting the other one on. The problem was that he was trying to put his tighty-whiteys on the other foot. We just watched and giggled. "What the hell! Where's my other sock?" I had a good idea where it was, and it probably wasn't very comfortable! He rushed back to the bedroom and redressed, socks on his feet, and undies on his butt.

PRANKSTER

Within minutes he was out the door and headed to the coffee shop to prank his buddies. Before walking into the shop, Dad put on a Willie Nelson wig and a pair of dark sunglasses. When he walked in, four of his old buddies were doing the regular rolling of dice for coffee. It's amazing how excited they would get when the loser had to buy a round of coffee for the gang.

Dad pulled up a seat next to Louie, one of his best old friends. Louie was a pretty straight-laced kind of guy, and old hippies were not his favorite type. Dad didn't say many words, just some hm's and ha's. He'd point and make goofy gestures with his arms. He had them all a bit uneasy, especially Louie. He was as close to Louie as could be without being in his lap. Before long, Louie had approached his boiling point and was about ready to knock this old hippie off his stool! Dad took off his glasses and smiled at Louie.

"Bert, you son of a bitch! I almost knocked you on your ass!" The whole coffee shop was in hysterics. Dad almost peed his pants. He'd succeeded in another great prank.

Stink Boat

DAD PASSED HIS love of pranks on to his kids, and we passed the gene on to ours. This morning, I had my daughter, Julie, helping me on the boat. At that time, Julie was nineteen years old. She was a good hand on the boat and always a customer favorite. We were drinking coffee and waiting on the boat for our charter clients to show up.

At 6:00 a.m., three gentlemen appeared at the top of the ramp. They were looking down at the boats, turning in circles, not knowing in which boat they were going fishing. My innocent little girl had a mischievous twinkle in her eyes, "Dad, I'm sure that's our charter, and I think we need to start the morning off with a good prank!"

I didn't want to, but how could I say no to my little girl? Up the ramp we went to gather up our morning victims. After handshakes and introductions, we headed back down the ramp to a different boat. We marched them down to the ugliest, filthiest, most stinky skiff in the harbor. She was a fifteen-foot flat-bottom crab skiff with no cabin. The boat had a fifty-gallon garbage can in the middle of it, filled with three- or four-day-old herring and salmon carcasses for crab bait. These guys were all smiles and grins until we stopped at the stink boat.

I said, "Well guys, she's not the prettiest boat in the fleet, but she catches fish!" Smiles immediately turned to panicked frowns. This was not the Alaskan adventure they'd been dreaming of.

Julie looked at the three traumatized gentlemen and smiled from ear to ear. "This isn't really the boat. Ours is that nice one with the big warm cabin on it." Frowns turned back to smiles. Everyone laughed all day about the morning prank.

At the end of a great day of fishing, the guys requested we do a prank the next morning on their buddy Brian who would be joining the group. The three of them also wanted to be accomplices to the prank. I wanted no part of it, but Julie and the guys made me do it.

The next morning it was basically the same setup. Same stinky boat, and still the same stinky garbage can full of old bait. Today was an ugly, rainy, windy morning. Julie and I were dressed in full rain gear. To up my pranking game, I had tucked a rusty old gaff hook up my raincoat sleeve so that only the hook was showing outside the sleeve. At 6:00 a.m. sharp, our three accomplices and their pigeon were marching down the dock.

Julie and I were positioned at the stink boat. You could hear the group talking and laughing about their fishing stories from the previous day. They had Brian all jacked up and filled with excitement. Around the corner they came, and there we were awaiting the group and their new member, Brian.

Brian was definitely not a fisherman. He looked like he was going to board a cruise ship rather than a fishing boat. He was dressed in tan khaki slacks and a sweater. One of the guys looked at Brian and said, "Well, here we are. This is our captain and his first mate Julie Kay."

Brian took a look at us and then looked down at the stink boat. The look on his face was priceless. He looked like a kid who had walked in on his parents having sex! I walked up to him and extended my hook to shake his hand. "I'm Captain Dan, nice to meet you." Brian gently grabbed the hook with two fingers and shook, hand and hook. He bought it all the way.

Brian looked down at the boat again, "Well, that's quite the boat. My partners say you catch fish though, so I'm game for anything!"

"Great," I said, "I'll need you and Julie sitting as far forward of the garbage can as possible, and the other three of you just behind the can." Brian carefully began to climb aboard the stink boat. When he looked up, we were all smiling, and then came the laughter. Julie

STINK BOAT

led Brian to the real *Julie Kay*. Compared to the stink boat, this boat looked like a cruise ship to Brian.

This had become one of my favorite pranks, but every once in a while, a prank backfired. I tried the stink boat prank on an old codger and his wife one morning. I led them to the little stinky boat. "Here we are. She's not the prettiest boat in the fleet, but she catches fish!" The old codger's wife was appalled.

The old codger took a look at the boat and then looked at me. "Son, we've got us a real problem. I didn't come no two thousand God damned miles to go out fishing on a flat-bottom, stinking boat."

I had picked the wrong guy to prank. He wanted my head at this point. "Whoa, whoa," I said sheepishly, "this really isn't our boat, we are over there."

His wife started laughing, "He really had you going!" I couldn't backpedal out of that prank fast enough!

My prankster daughter Julie Kay

The Meeting

IT WAS EARLY June and the king salmon season was swinging into gear. We would begin the day jigging fresh herring. Everyone loves catching herring. It can be a challenge to make people stop, especially kids. Once the bait was caught, it was off to the king salmon grounds.

The king salmon fishing had really picked up in the last three days, and today would not disappoint. Within the first hour, we had two nice kings in the box and had multiple strikes.

Midway through the morning, I noticed an aluminum boat with a jet black cabin trolling down the bank. It was a boat I'd never seen around Petersburg. I began to notice that the more action we were getting, the closer the black boat was narrowing. By midafternoon, we were fishing for one more king to limit the boat out. Throughout the day, the black boat shadowed us, but I never did see any excitement on the boat. Finally, the boat fired up its engine and headed for town. It almost looked like he was tired of seeing us catch fish.

For the next few days, the salmon fishing continued to be excellent. Another thing that continued was the black aluminum boat fishing alongside me, or right behind me. The boat soon got the nickname, "my shadow." Everywhere I fished, the black boat fished. If I pulled up the lines to move a quarter mile, I had a black boat right behind me. From a distance, you would swear I was towing him. I really did have a shadow.

The boat looked to have an older fella and a lady on board. I would look over with my binoculars to try to see what was going on aboard the black boat, and occasionally I would look over to see a pair of binoculars looking back at me. The couple must have trailered the boat to Petersburg. They were definitely not locals. You could tell the poor guy was getting more and more frustrated each day. The fishermen on the boat right next to him was catching their limit of salmon day after day, and his rods remained limp. His patience was getting shorter and shorter. He would fire up the black boat and head back to town earlier each day.

It was obvious I was doing something totally different than he was. The little black boat was trolling in front of me, beside me, and behind me, and I don't think he got as much as a strike in three days. We were catching fish all around the poor couple. Singles, doubles, and even a triple-header! It had been another successful day of king salmon fishing for us. Again, the man fired up the engine and the black boat headed to town.

After the third day of being followed, I pulled my boat into her slip, and there was an older man sitting in a chair right where I tied the boat lines to their cleats. The man sat and watched, one leg crossed over the other very comfortably. My charter clients got off the boat, and I unloaded their catch. The man just watched but remained silent. After finishing up cleaning the fish, I returned to the boat to clean up and put my poles away. The older fella was still there, sitting in the chair, one leg crossed over the other with his head tilted down. I asked him if I could help him with something. I had no idea why this man was silently sitting beside my boat.

The gentleman slowly raised his head and began to speak, "Young man, my name is Arley Haener, from Grangeville, Idaho. I'm not a young man anymore, I don't have much patience, and at my age I don't have that much time for learning to fish all over again. Now, I've been watching you catch those salmon all week and, young man, you are going to teach me how to fish!"

Now, it all made sense. It was the man in the black boat, my shadow. He even knew where I parked my boat! Before I could respond,

THE MEETING

Mr. Arley Haener stepped onto my boat. He grabbed his chair, opened up his cooler, and pulled out two plastic glasses and a fifth of Crown Royal. He proceeded to fill our glasses half full of whiskey.

I liked this guy already. How couldn't you? He was one of a kind. We took a couple sips of Crown and then Arley broke into his cooler again, and this time, out came a handful of salmon leaders and a pack of herring. "Now," he said, "let's see how we put these sardines on the hooks." He was completely serious. I could not believe it!

"Now hold on here a minute before you show me your tricks. I'm going to get Irene." Arley's wife, Irene, had been just down the dock, while Arley was working his magic. Within five minutes, Arley and Irene stepped onto my boat.

Irene was a beautiful woman. She had beautiful white hair and a warm, wonderful smile. Irene immediately began apologizing for Arley's tactics. She was a real sweetheart. How Arley got ahold of her, I'll never know.

"Okay, okay, okay, now let's see how we put these sardines on the hooks," Arley stammered.

I looked at the leaders and saw Arley's first problem. The leaders were one-hundred-pound tests. "Nope," I told him. "These won't work; they are way too heavy." Irene and Arley spent most of their winters in Cabo San Lucas, Mexico, and were accustomed to fishing with big poles and heavy leaders. Arley's tackle was not going to work in these waters.

I grabbed some leaders out of the cabin and began class. First, I instructed them on how to thread a whole herring. Arley continuously told Irene, "Pay attention. You have got to learn how to do this, Irene." Irene just nodded and reassured Arley that she could do it. It was becoming more and more obvious that only one student was paying attention. Arley was busy making sure my glass was kept full. After rigging multiple baits, I asked if they would like to give it a try.

"No, no," Arley said, "we'll just keep these ones you have already done, and we can just copy your work."

Next, I showed them how to rig a cut plug, by far the easiest bait to rig. I knew Irene would have no problems with this one. Arley pleaded, "Now pay attention, Irene. Did you get it? You've got to remember how to rig these sardines!"

Irene just smiled. "Yes, Arley." Irene was going to pass my class, and the only reason Arley would pass was because he never let his teacher's glass become empty.

Arley gathered all the baits I had rigged up and gently laid them in his cooler. The Haeners were baited up and ready to catch a king in the morning. I guess he figured if Irene forgot how to do it, they already had ten rigs in the cooler ready to go. Arley knew every trick! I had a really good idea where they would be fishing tomorrow and looked forward to seeing them right next to me, hopefully catching a fish this time.

Little did I know, this day would be one of the luckiest days of my life. I had just met two wonderful people who would become very close to me and my family.

Blame Game

THE NEXT MORNING, I had four new clients. We jigged our herring and we were on our way to hopefully have a good day of king salmon fishing. Right behind me was the black aluminum boat with my new friends, Arley and Irene Haener.

Twenty minutes later, as we arrived at our fishing spot, I began getting the gear in the water. Before I could put the last rod in the water, we had a fish on. I could hear Arley, just off the side of our boat, "Irene, they've already got a fish on and we haven't even got our bait in the water!" Within fifteen minutes, we had already landed our first fish. It was going to be a good day.

I was keeping a close eye on Arley and Irene. I wanted to witness my pupils landing their first king salmon. Thirty minutes later, another nice salmon came aboard our boat. By noon we had five. The bite was on…for our boat.

Poor Arley was beside himself. We were catching fish all around the black boat, but still not even a strike for the Haeners. I was so confident they would catch a fish. Their bait was good, they looked to be trolling the right speed, and there were lots of fish in the area. It just didn't make sense not to even get a bite.

I could see Arley pacing back and forth, cursing his limp and lifeless poles. "Irene, what are we doing wrong?" He would bring up the downriggers and stare into the water at the baits, then back down they would go. He looked over at me with his arms out as if to say, "What the hell am I doing wrong?" Then we caught one right behind him and that was the last straw. The black boat fired up her engine and away the Haeners headed for the barn.

When I returned to my stall a couple hours later, Arley was sitting in the same place as the day before. He immediately put the blame on Irene for not paying attention to the baiting and trolling techniques I had taught the night before. "It's just not possible that you could catch eight salmon, and we were only twenty-five yards away and couldn't even get a bite! She must have forgotten something you told us." I agreed that it didn't seem possible, and I didn't have an answer. As far as he was concerned, it couldn't possibly be his fault. It had to be Irene's. Irene was a great sport and was always there to take the blame. In Arley's mind, he was always right. After he was finished blaming his lovely wife, he invited me over for one of Irene's special Bloody Marys. Come to find out, they were staying in a travel trailer just two blocks from our house. The couple had driven their mobile home, with boat in tow, from their home in Idaho to Seattle, Washington, and then taken the state ferry to Petersburg.

After I cleaned the boat, I stopped by the Haener's trailer. Irene greeted me with her perfect smile and the best Bloody Mary I had ever tasted. "Okay," Arley began, "let's get down to business. You caught eight kings today, and we didn't even get a bite. It's obvious you're doing something different than us."

Arley was right, but I didn't know what it was without actually fishing with him. I could only imagine what his rigged herring looked like before I changed the leaders he was using and taught him how to bait a herring. With a one-hundred-pound test line and great big hooks in a little herring, he didn't have a prayer of a salmon biting. I told Arley and Irene that the only difference I could think of was that I was using fresh-caught herring, and they were using store-bought frozen herring. I was a bit skeptical if fresh bait was going to make the difference, but it was worth a try.

I finished my second Bloody Mary and got a big hug from Irene and headed home. One of Irene's Bloody Marys was perfect, but two and I needed to walk home. They packed a serious punch! I hoped the Haeners would give it another try tomorrow with some fresh bait.

Quick Study

THE NEXT MORNING, the Haeners stopped by my boat with leaders and freshly caught herring. Arley wanted another lesson on rigging his herring before heading out fishing. I rigged a fillet, a plug, and a whole herring. The two of them studied every detail. "Irene, are you paying attention? You need to know how to do this," Arley stammered. After rigging the baits, I asked Arley to rig one. I wanted to see what a Haener bait looked like.

The mystery of why the Haeners were getting skunked was soon starting to make sense. Arley grabbed a herring to rig. Oh my God! He put the hooks in the bait and then pulled them out and put them in another way. Then the herring squirted out of his hands and onto the deck. He picked it up and reinserted the hooks a third time. After the five-minute massacre of his herring, he was done. "There, is that right, Dan?"

I've heard of fish biting on hot dogs because they were so hungry, but Arley's mangled creation had absolutely no chance. I looked at Arley's mess and could only shake my head. If he was planning on pickling his herring, it was a great job. His bait was completely mangled and scaleless. Every scale was on the deck or on Arley. Irene watched and just smiled quietly. Arley then tried his hand at rigging a plug and a fillet, both with the same outcomes of mushy, mangled messes of baits.

Now it was Irene's turn. She gently grabbed a herring and slipped the hooks through the nose, flipped the bait over and positioned both hooks in the bait in the back. She had rigged a perfect herring, all scales intact. Irene was a quick learner. Arley, on the other hand, well, let's just say, he tried hard.

We soon headed out, back to the same area that had been producing good salmon fishing. My shadow was right behind me with newly born confidence and fresh bait. As long as Arley left the baiting to Irene, I felt the chances of catching a king on the F/V *Miss Irene* were looking really good.

By 7:00 a.m., we had arrived at our fishing spot. The fishing was slow this morning. After two hours without even a strike, I decided to pull up the gear and change locations. I moved about four miles down the bank and put the lines back in. While trolling along the shore, I noticed herring being rushed to the surface in a little cove just ahead of us in. I shallowed the lines up and maneuvered into the cove. As soon as I got into the cove and turned the boat to head out of it, *bam!* A rod tip bent toward the water. Just as one client grabbed the rod, another rod went off on the other side of the boat. We had a doubleheader! The morning had started off slow but was heating up fast. Within twenty minutes, we had a thirty- and a thirty-five-pound king on board.

I ran the boat back fifty yards from the little cove and trolled back through the same spot and *wham!*...fish on again!...another beautiful king of about twenty pounds. The feed was hanging out in this little cove and so were the kings.

I continued to run back fifty yards from the cove, reset the gear and *boom!* This little cove was loaded with king salmon. By 2:00 p.m., we had our limit of kings ranging from twenty to forty pounds.

Arley and Irene were just trolling down the bank when I netted the final king.

It had been another uneventful morning on the F/V *Miss Irene*. Arley was doing his back-and-forth pacing, arms in the air with disgust, and a whole lot of "*I-rene!*"

I had the same group as the day before, and they tried not to laugh, but there was a lot of humor coming out of Arley's pain. "Irene, it's not possible. I mean, not possible. There's just got to be one dumb fish down there!" we could hear him shout. Watching Arley pace and do all of his other gyrations while Irene just quietly sat and enjoyed the day was humorous, but I really felt bad that they couldn't catch a fish.

The last four fish we had caught all came out of a little area in the cove, right alongside some big rocks protruding out of the water. I pulled alongside Arley and Irene, pointed out the little cove, and told them to troll in there. I backed off and watched as they trolled in and out of the cove with not so much as a bite. Arley was beside himself.

I had an idea, one last-ditch effort. The last four fish had been caught in the same spot, and with the same flasher too. I pulled my boat alongside Arley and Irene. "Okay," I said, "let's try this." I took Arley's setup off his pole. My God! That was the most pathetic-looking concoction I'd ever seen, and I definitely did not teach them how to rig a herring like that in class. I think the reason we were catching all the fish was because Arley was scaring them to us.

I put my super-duper flasher with a prebaited herring on Arley's rod. I then instructed Irene to troll right by the big rocks. My first instruction for Arley was, "Don't touch the bait." Some people give off a bad scent that fish don't like, and Arley was surely one of those people. Next, I had Arley trail the super duper about twelve feet behind the boat, and then attach it to his downrigger and slowly, gently drop it down to forty-five feet. "Guaranteed," I said, "You can't miss!" My clients were in stitches, watching this show.

Arley bet me a dinner that there would be no fish. Irene trolled their boat down the bank. I motored along at a short distance away so all could see and hear. I had no idea what masterpiece Arley had trolling on the other rod he had out. I was just hoping it wouldn't scare the fish away from the super duper. Irene steered the boat next to the rocks and then began her swing into the little cove. Arley was hovering directly over the pole, giving it a serious stare-down and talking to it, "I just dare you. C'mon, make my day!"

Around the corner and into the cove the F/V *Miss Irene* went, and just as Irene was turning out, *ka-wham-o*…down went the rod! At first, Arley jumped back. He looked like the guy who had just gotten the crap scared out of him in a horror movie. We could hear Irene shout, "Arley, Arley!"

Arley grabbed the rod, still in total disbelief. The folks on my boat were all cheering Arley on. Arley looked at his reel as the line was flying out of it, "Irene, I've got one!" In sheer panic, he began tightening the drag, and then it was over, just as fast as it began. *Snap* went the line, and Arley's rod went limp. "Irene," he yelled, "what did I do that for?"

Not only did he lose the first fish in a week but he lost my one-of-a-kind super-duper flasher! I idled over next to the Haeners to hear Arley say, "You don't really think that was a salmon, do you?" The Arley and Irene show was becoming the highlight of my charters. Arley was not going to be a quick study in the art of catching a king salmon.

I stopped by the Haener's with Cheryl and the kids later that afternoon. Irene made us one of her special Bloody Marys. Arley had been downtown searching for a super-duper flasher like the one he had lost, but he came up empty-handed. I told him it was a one-of-a-kind original. It really wasn't, but I sure did get a kick out of watching the old codger stir.

We drank our drinks and laughed about Arley and the king that got away with my super duper. Little Scottie and Julie had soon set up camp at the kitchen table, and Irene taught them how to play a card game called four-cornered kings. Irene had instantly become a favorite with the kids. Even though technically Arley did not catch a salmon, I still held him to a dinner.

Fog

THE SALMON FISHING remained good for the month of June. Irene caught multiple kings throughout the month, and after many failures, I finally got Arley his first king salmon. My mission had been accomplished.

As the king salmon fishing slowed, most of my charters had turned to halibut. The Haeners fished for halibut close to town but occasionally would follow me out farther to the areas I fished. They would always check with me to make sure I didn't mind. Arley and Irene's boat was a bit smaller than mine but plenty big if the weather was decent.

Halibut fishing was the perfect type of fishing for Arley. Once you had one hooked, they were pretty tough to lose, even for Arley. This morning, the Haeners followed me to a spot I'd taken them halibut fishing before. It was going to be a calm day, so I agreed.

We began running out to the halibut hole. About three miles into the trip, we ran into heavy fog. I radioed Arley, told him to stay close to me, and continued on through the dense fog. I'd done it a hundred times.

Back in those days, we didn't have the luxury of GPS to rely on to guide you to wherever you wanted to go. I had a depth sounder, my compass, a watch, and I knew all the rocks and landmarks to get me to my fishing spots. Arley continued to call me on the radio, "Young man," he'd say, "are you sure we are going in the right direction?"

I would reassure him that we were definitely heading the right direction. About every ten minutes the radio would blare, "Young man, you have no idea where we are!" Then, "You've done a complete circle, and we are going the opposite direction you think we are!"

This went on for about an hour—Arley calling on the radio every ten minutes and me responding to reassure him that I knew exactly where we were and to stay within my view.

My passengers heard him and laughed. Thank God, they had confidence in me. The fog never budged the entire trip out. If anything, it got worse. All Arley could see was my shadow, and he was not going to let me out of his sight, even if he thought I was lost.

After about an hour and a half, I knew we were getting close to where I needed to change course to get to the fishing spot. I headed the boat close to the shore until I could just make out a big rock on the beach. This was the landmark I was looking for. Then, I turned the boat to my desired compass course and ran at 25 mph for twenty minutes heading offshore. We were now very close.

I kept watching the depth sounder, and then the depth began to shallow rapidly to six hundred feet, four hundred feet, and up to one hundred sixty feet. We were at the halibut hole. Over the anchor went. This is where we would fish.

Arley put his anchor down just off to the side of us, just barely in view, but in great hearing range. We could hear everything he said. "Irene, he has no idea where we are and I mean, no idea!" Arley was convinced we were about forty miles from where we wanted to be.

I baited up the gear, and we were fishing. Arley and Irene were now out of sight in the fog, but in perfect listening range. "Irene, how the hell are we ever going to get home?" Arley hated fog. I don't like fog either, but normally if you have dense fog, you have calm weather. Once you get to where you want to fish, it's fine, and it usually lifts by noon and becomes a beautiful day.

Within minutes, one of the gals on my boat hooked a nice halibut. There was lots of squealing and grunting as she worked the fish to the boat. Five minutes later, I cracked the aluminum bat over a nice forty-pound halibut's head.

DROPPING MY LINES

Ready to bonk a halibut between the eyes

The other poles began jumping into action. This spot had been producing day after day, and it looked like today would be another action-packed day. We could hear the Haeners laughing as they both

FOG

fought a fish. "Can you believe this, Irene? He doesn't have a clue where he is and he still found fish!" Arley was still convinced we were miles and miles away from where I thought we were.

The fog slowly began to break around 11:00 a.m., and the mountains and shoreline began to come into view. We all had a perfect view of Arley. He looked one way, then turned and looked another way. Pretty soon we could hear him say, "Irene, it's not possible, and I mean not possible! He's got us on the exact spot he said we were on! How did he do that?"

Irene laughed and said, "I had no doubt in my mind." It turned out to be another successful day of fishing for both us and the Haeners, and best of I all, I made Arley eat a little crow!

Great Lifestyle

IT DIDN'T TAKE long before Arley and Irene became more than just fishing friends. Our two kids loved to be around them. The Destroyer, (Scottie), must have been about six years old, and The Informer, (Julie), was about eight years old when the Haener's first came to Petersburg. I think Scott spent as much time in their travel trailer as he did at home. We would frequently get phone calls from Irene letting us know Scott had peddled his bike over to their place and that they were playing their favorite game, four-cornered kings. They would keep a running tally of how many games each of them had won all summer long. Scott was Irene's little buddy.

The Haener residence soon became a daily stop for the kids and Cheryl. I made it a must stop after charters—I had to have one of Irene's Bloody Marys. Scottie's little red bike would almost always be there when I stopped by.

Arley would usually be cooking crab or smoking fish in his Little Chief smoker. He smoked up the collars, tips, and fins of the salmon. I would always save these salmon parts for Arley. God knows he would starve if he relied on his own success at catching salmon. Arley loved crab and smoked salmon, but he did not like eating regular fish. He liked to fish but was not a fish eater, unless it was a greasy piece of smoked fish.

GREAT LIFESTYLE

Scottie at his second home

As the summers came and went, the Haeners kept with the same schedule.

Arley and Irene spent June, July, and August in Petersburg. They loved Petersburg, and every June, the Haener's returned. Petersburg became their second home, and we couldn't wait for them to return each summer.

When they left in August, they went back to their home in Grangeville, Idaho, for part of the winter, and then took off to Cabo

San Lucas, Mexico, where they wintered for a few months. Arley and Irene also had a boat in Cabo—an aluminum boat with a black hardtop cabin, just like the one in Petersburg. They truly were enjoying life.

The two became quite popular with many of my charter clients. It was a regular occurrence to have the black aluminum boat anchor within rock-throwing distance of the *Julie Kay*. Arley would yell over at me, "Hey, young man, what do you think you're doing following me to my halibut hole!" The entertainment would then begin. Not only were my clients having fun catching halibut on my boat, but they got to watch Captain Arley and First Mate Irene fish on their boat too. There was never a dull moment on the *Miss Irene*.

We could hear the captain giving instructions. "Irene, what are you doing?" Or "Irene, are you on the bottom?" Then, "Irene, are you sure you have bait on?"

Needless to say, Arley was usually the one who was baitless or not on the bottom. Halibut fishing was perfect for Arley, as it didn't take much skill to catch the flat fish. Once you figured out where they were, it was just a matter of getting your bait to the bottom and letting the fish hook themselves. Almost any bait would work, and the bait didn't need to be put on the hook in any special way. It was the perfect stupid fish for Arley.

Irene would hook a halibut, and everyone on the boat could hear Captain Arley giving her instructions. She would just smile and say, "Yes, Arley." If it was a decent-sized fish, Arley would get his sawed-off .410 shotgun.

"Okay," he'd say, "just get his head to the surface." Before he would shoot, I'd tell my clients to get down or take cover. Irene would lift the fish's head just to the surface and *ka-boom*, Arley would start giggling like a kid. "Look at that, I really laid him out." My whole boat would be in hysterics watching the show.

We visited the Haeners in Cabo in the winter and went fishing with the two of them for dorado, wahoo, marlin, or anything that would bite. Having a black cabin on your boat in Cabo...holy crap,

GREAT LIFESTYLE

you talk about hot! We also fished out of Arley and Irene's close friends, Alter and Cathy's, boat. They also had small children, and the Haeners had a similar relationship with them as with our family. What a great life…summers in Petersburg, Alaska, winters in Cabo San Lucas, Mexico. They had fishing and friends in both places. It doesn't get much better than that! Throughout the next fifteen years, there would be many wonderful times and unforgettable memories with the Haeners.

Plow Bait

IT HAD BEEN over a week of salmon trolling, and the Haeners were still fishless. I had a day off and invited them to go king salmon fishing with me, and hopefully get them on the right path to catching a king. They gladly accepted. It had become my personal goal to get Arley Haener a king salmon.

We started the regular morning ritual of herring jigging. Irene was the jigger, Arley was Mr. Bait Boy, and I was the driver. I was a little concerned about the way the bait boy was getting the herring off the hooks. Arley would grab the herring, and the fish would wiggle and squirt out of Arley's paw. He'd grab the herring again, and finally after completely violating the herring, the scaleless, tainted fish would go into the bucket. After watching Arley massacre about twenty herring, I began quickly shaking a few herring into a separate container. I am very superstitious when it comes to trolling for kings. Just the thought of having Arley's smell on the bait gave out bad vibes. Soon we had a bucket of Arley's mangled bait and a small container of nice herring that had been untouched by Mr. Bait Boy.

Arley was covered in herring scales. Even his nose had scales on it. I think he actually had more scales on him than his entire bucket had in it. We had our fresh bait, and it was off to catch a king salmon.

Twenty minutes later, we arrived at our fishing spot, and I began baiting up the first herring. Irene took over driving, and it was the two boys on the deck working the salmon gear. Arley paid close attention as I rigged the bait and then slowly dropped it to forty feet on the

PLOW BAIT

downrigger. As I put it in the water to see how it looked, Arley said, "Is it supposed to roll like that?"

"Yes," I replied. "If I was a king salmon, I would grab that thing in a heartbeat."

Now it was Arley's turn to rig up his bait. Just as Arley began his baiting process, Irene started pointing and yelling, "Fish, fish!" Sure enough, we had a fish on the line I had just put down. Arley looked at the bouncing rod in disbelief.

"That's just not possible!" he yelled. Arley grabbed the pole, and the fight was on. I reminded Arley to be patient, not to mess with the drag, and to keep his thumb off the line. Let the rod and reel tire the fish out, and then you can gently start bringing the fish closer to the boat. There are two words that were not in Arley's vocabulary: *patient* and *gently*. The fish made a quick run at the boat, shook his head, and he was gone. Arley was holding a limp rod again. Another king salmon had outfoxed Arley. There really wasn't much Arley could have done; the fish just got away. Yes, that's why it's called fishing.

Quickly, I baited up again and got the line back in the water. Now was the moment of truth: time for Arley to bait a herring. He grabbed a herring out of his bucket and flipped it back and forth about five times, trying to decide which side he was going to begin threading his hooks through. Finally, after almost tearing the nose off the herring, he had the hooks threaded through.

"Okay," I told him, "now flip the herring over and *gently* put the hooks in the other side." Arley rolled his bait fish over and put the hooks in the herring backward. I shook my head. "Try putting them in the opposite direction." Out came the hooks, and back into the limp, mushy herring the hooks went. It was painful to watch. He was trying so hard, yet doing so badly. "Okay," I said, "Now *gently* put a half hitch around the nose, and you've got it." I helped him with the final half hitch before he completely destroyed his creation.

Arley was so proud of his bait. I just couldn't hurt his feelings and tell him what I really thought. He dropped his offering into the water to see what kind of action it had. "Well," he said, "what do you think?"

This was definitely the most miserable-looking herring I'd ever seen. It had zero scales, half of its side was gone from repositioning hooks over and over, and the once-firm herring was now mushy. The herring looked beat up and mangled. We both looked at Arley's pathetic bait in the water. It just plowed beneath the surface. It looked like an overweight water skier failing to get up on top of the water. I kept hoping it would magically make some sort of a roll. I had Irene speed the boat up to see if we could get some sort of movement out of it. Not a chance. The plow bait would not spin, roll, or turn; it just plowed through the water.

I had to be honest with Arley, so I told him his bait did not have a chance in hell. It was very obvious to me now why the Haeners had not caught a salmon. I suggested we try a plug-cut herring instead. Just cut the head off at an angle, take out the guts, one hook in the tail section, one hook forward, and if it spins, rolls, or moves in any way, we will call it good. I was losing my patience and just wanted to get the line in the water.

Irene continued trolling down the bank, smiling while she listened to the student and teacher. Arley grabbed another herring out of his bucket and laid it on the cutting board. He then flipped his fish back and forth, trying to decide how he wanted to cut the head off. I drew an imaginary line with the angle I wanted on the herring, and Arley made the cut. Then he began trying to get the guts out. *"Gently,"* I said. "You don't have to tear the belly out to get the guts out."

After fondling the poor bait for five minutes, it was time to put it in the water to see if it made any kind of a roll, wiggle, or spin. Arley put his mangled creation into the water and watched it plow through the water. The bait plowed side to side, then would almost surface, and then plow downward. "What do you think?" Arley asked.

"Well, it's moving, so I guess it's got a chance." Who cared if it didn't have any scales? We attached the plow bait to the downrigger and dropped it down. I had zero confidence in Arley's bait, but we still had one good bait fishing and our chances were good.

I suggested that Arley fish the rod he baited and Irene fish the other rod. We needed to catch a fish, and I wasn't very confident in Arley actually getting one in the boat. On the other hand, I was very confident nothing was going to touch his plow bait.

We trolled for about an hour before a line came to life. It was the line on the opposite side of Arley's plow bait. Arley grabbed Irene's pole and began playing the fish. I got the other pole and downriggers out of the way. I began reinforcing the word *gentle* to Arley. He wasn't the gentlest person I'd seen with a rod. He had a bad habit of jerking the fish right back whenever it jerked. "Easy," I'd say, "if the fish is jerking his head back and forth, there's nothing you can do. Just hold the rod and don't jerk back."

It looked as though Arley was going to land his first king salmon. The fish was just about played out but then made one last run and a jump. When a fish jumps out of the water, the natural tendency is to pull or jerk your rod. The correct move, though, is to bow your rod to the fish as it lands back in the water, so there is no extra tension on the line. Arley went with the natural tendency. The fish jumped and Arley jerked.

When the fish hit the water, he was free. The hooks had pulled out. So close, but the third time wasn't a charm. Arley was disgusted. "What did I do wrong?"

I explained the trick of bowing the rod. Arley just nodded his head. It was obvious we needed a salmon to get hooked so well that he would just surrender. My personal mission of getting Arley his first king salmon was going to take a whole lot of patience.

Arley demanded that if another fish hit, it would be Irene's. That sounded like a great idea. I rigged another bait, Arley put his scaleless wonder back in the water, and we were trolling again. If he was preparing the herring for pickling, he was doing an excellent job.

Over the next two hours, we had a couple strikes but no good hookups. A couple strikes on my side of the boat, that is. Arley was still trolling his original ugly, untouched plug.

Finally, one of the rods took off! (not Arley's) This fish was hooked and taking line. Arley cleared his line, and I got the downriggers up and out of the way. Irene grabbed the pole and just held it steady while the king made his first initial run. The salmon slowed and then ran back at the boat. Irene quickly and calmly collected the line back on her reel that she had lost on the fish's first run. The salmon stopped and began shaking his head back and forth. Irene held the rod steady, waiting for the salmon's next move.

I watched a thing of beauty—no jerking, no messing with the drag, no sudden movements with the rod. This beautiful, white-haired lady was an absolute pro! She was so smooth and gentle with every movement, as not to disturb the hooks in the salmon's mouth. Irene, slowly and patiently, wore the salmon down until it rolled on its side, and then she guided the fish perfectly into the net!

I was amazed. Irene did everything with perfection. Irene had caught her first king salmon…a beautiful twenty-five pounder. Arley's beautiful wife was all smiles. It was such a wonderful sight to see Irene smile while she talked to her fish and methodically wore it down. It was obvious she had done a lot of fishing in her life. Irene Haener was one hell of a fisherman. It may have been her first king salmon, but it looked like she'd been catching kings all her life. Irene was such a natural that I felt like I was the student and she was the teacher. Arley, on the other hand, was a disaster when it came to king salmon fishing. And I mean a "DISASTER!"

Meanwhile, Arley had reeled in his plug, and to his surprise, it was gone. "And you were making fun of *my* bait!" Arley was convinced that something had eaten his bait. I let him believe he had a strike. A student can only take so much criticism in one day. I am fairly certain that his plow bait was so water logged and soggy that it couldn't hang on anymore and had eventually just fallen off. It was a good way to end a day—Arley had a "strike" on his own bait, and Irene caught her first king.

Arley's Big Fish

LIKE MOST JULY mornings, the weather was nice. It had become common to have my shadow trailing close behind on the way to the halibut grounds. Everyone listened to Arley on the radio. It always started with, "Young man, we travel twenty-five to thirty miles to catch a halibut. Now you can't tell me there's no halibut somewhere in between, maybe a little closer to town?"

I'd tell him he was right, there are closer halibut, but I don't want to waste my time trying to find them there when I can just run another half hour to where I know they are.

Then he'd usually end his conversation with, "So, how many people are you taking to the cleaners today?" Arley had my clients and me rolling with laughter. He pulled off quite a show!

Everyone got to catch plenty of fish and keep a couple of nice-sized halibut. The biggest fish today though was hooked on the F/V *Miss Irene*. My charter clients were in for some great Haener entertainment!

Irene would bring a thirty-pound halibut up, and Arley would throw a harpoon through it. Sometimes it would take a few tries. Once harpooned, he would take out his bat and begin bashing the poor fish over the head, over and over and over. Arley's magic number was thirty-five whacks to the head. I would tell my customers that he was going to club that fish thirty-five times. They would begin counting, and sure enough, thirty-five whacks to the head was the number. I'd seen Arley in action before, and it was always thirty-five, every time, nothing less, nothing more.

Arley was pooped by the time he finished beating the fish. My group was in tears watching the production. We were having a good day of fishing, and I think our fishing was being over shadowed by the entertainment we were witnessing on the black boat.

Soon after Irene's fish was in the boat, Arley jumped up out of his chair, grabbed his rod, and began jerking his rod to set the hook. I've told Arley a hundred times not to set the hook with circle hooks, but my pupil never listened to me. The fish was evidently already hooked before Arley began trying to rip its lips off. It was a big one. Arley's pole doubled over. When it came to fishing gear, the Haeners used the best on the market. Their poles were specially handcrafted, and the reels were big, beautiful two-speed Shimanos spooled with one-hundred-pound test line. Arley jerked his rod back with every jerk the fish made. Thank God halibut are hard to lose once they're hooked… the opposite of salmon.

We all watched and listened to the general bark orders. "Irene! I've got Moby Butt on! Get your line out of the water so you don't tangle me up!"

Irene managed their top-of-the-line fighting belt around Arley's waist, and the butt of the rod snapped into its place on the belt. Arley was now ready for battle. This fish was giving Arley the fight of his life.

After half an hour, the fish was tiring. She must have been hooked well because Mr. Finesse had jerked on her every which way but loose. Irene was such a natural, and Arley was a natural disaster (sorry Arley) when it came to finesse. Arley had gained all the line back that the halibut had taken. Now the real work began. The big fish was slowly being lifted from the bottom. Arley was really feeling the weight of the bruiser now. He yelled at us, "I think I've snagged onto a Volkswagen!"

After a long battle, the fish was almost to the surface. "Irene," Arley said, "get me my snake charmer!" In the cabin she went, and seconds later came back toting a sawed off .410 shotgun. Arley meant business. He gave the pole to Irene and took the gun. "Okay, now

Irene, you bring him up just so his head hits the top of the water, and I'm gonna flatten this kid right out."

Everybody on my boat was all eyes and ears. I told everyone to get behind something solid. Irene slowly coaxed the big halibut to the surface. Arley took aim and *ka-boom*…water went flying straight up in the air, and the big, flat fish took off running, running on the surface of the water like a salmon. Arley had shot a little prematurely, before the halibut's head had surfaced. He had knocked the fish cuckoo.

Arley put the gun down and grabbed the rod from Irene. The dingy fish ran on the surface almost to the side of my boat and then turned around and headed right back at Arley, still on the surface. Arley had really rung its bell and now had to reel in line as fast as he could while the fish swam toward the boat. The halibut didn't know up from down. The shell-shocked fish ran at the black boat and right under it. When it came out the other side, yes, shit hit the fan!

DROPPING MY LINES

Irene had reeled up her line but had left her hook barely hanging on the surface of the water. When the big halibut came out the other side, Irene's hook caught on the line as the fish passed by. The halibut was still on a dead run, and as soon as the line came tight, Irene's thousand-dollar fishing rod and reel went sling-shotting out into Frederick Sound. "I-rene! Irene! I told you!" Poor Irene. She did everything right; this couldn't possibly have just happened.

Finally, the halibut ran out of gas, and Arley began bringing the sucker back in. When he had him almost to the top, he handed Irene the rod again and he grabbed his trusty .410. Irene lifted the big fish's head just to the surface, and Arley blasted the bruiser again. This time, there was no movement. Arley had hit the spot.

He tied the fish off to the side of the boat. Arley looked at us with him arms spread out. "Can you believe that shit? That fish threw Irene's pole in the drink!" Arley and Irene both stood there looking at the big halibut, both soaking wet from the splash from Arley's gunshots in the water.

My group enjoyed the show of a lifetime, taking pictures of these two old farts and their huge fish hanging on the side of the boat. It couldn't have been scripted any better. "Hey, young man. Now what do I do? I can't lift this thing in the boat!" We pulled alongside and helped Arley drag his 225-pound halibut in the boat. "Just look at my fish," Arley said, "I will probably never catch a fish like that in my life. Hell, I can buy a new pole any time!" He was so right.

Arley's big fish

Can't Stop Time

SUMMER AFTER SUMMER, Arley and Irene returned to Petersburg. As the two aged, Arley in his eighties, and Irene not far behind, they began flying to Petersburg instead of bringing the travel trailer and boat. Arley and Irene began spending more time in Idaho, and less time in Petersburg and Cabo San Lucas. When they came to Petersburg, they would now just fish with me when I had a day off or extra space on my charters. The Haeners stayed at the Stockton's bed and breakfast. Time had begun to sneak up on them, and this system was much simpler. I would stop over often for my afternoon Bloody Mary and cook for them once in a while. The Stocktons became great friends and frequently joined in on cocktail hour as well. They always checked in on the Haeners to make sure all was okay and they were comfortable.

My return clients started requesting that I bring Arley and Irene along on my charters. I started thinking that maybe I should be paying the Haeners to go because people enjoyed them so much. Most of the time Arley wouldn't fish; he just liked to be part of the fun. When he did fish, he would purposely only let his line out about a quarter of the way to the bottom. Sometimes we could look over the side and see his bait just twenty feet down. This sure made bait checks easy for Arley.

Even in her later years, Irene loved to fish. She would fish every day if she could, and it didn't matter if the weather was nice or if it was nasty. She just loved to fish. Irene really was a fishing fool. Arley's back and legs gave him a lot of pain, and this limited the fishing time. He had caught lots of big fish and a couple of really stupid salmon in his time. It wasn't about catching fish anymore with Arley; he just wanted to watch his wife fish and enjoy herself.

As long as she had a pole in her arms, Irene couldn't be more content. I loved watching Irene fish. She always had to be holding the pole, slowly rocking it back and forth like a baby, and when a fish would bite, she would slowly pull away from it until it hooked itself. This beautiful, white-haired lady truly was the best fisherman I'd ever seen. She loved the feel of the bite. I'd watch her when she was getting a halibut bite. She would start talking to the fish, "Here we go, oh it tastes so good." She'd just tease the fish by slowly lifting her rod up and down, and then her rod would bend over, and the fish was hooked. Arley would strap her into the fighting belt, and the fight would be on. Irene almost never asked for help. She could almost always manage to finesse a big fish in.

One day after Irene had caught about a 150-pound halibut, Arley said, "If Irene ever hooks another big halibut, just let it go! These big flat fish are just too much work!" You'd think he was the one bringing them in. I agreed, let the big ones go. That sounded like a great idea to me.

Irene...Best fisherman.

Arley....Worst fisherman

Big, Big Fish!

THE MORNING BROUGHT rain, wind, and cold. On this nasty day, I had Arley, Irene, and a young Japanese man named Eugene on board for a day of halibut fishing. Eugene spoke very little English, hardly any at all. Eugene was like a kid, jigging up herring for bait. I could have just let him catch herring all day and it would have been the best fishing trip of his life. Arley was my first mate and "gently" took the herring off the herring jigs. As usual, by the time he was done, Arley had more scales on him than the herring had on them.

I headed out about twenty-five miles north into Frederick Sound. It took a bit longer to get to the fishing grounds due to the choppy water. Arley whined like a kid all the way. "Okay, now you can't tell me that there are no halibut between town and your halibut hole!" He grabbed a piece of paper and drew a line on a piece of paper. At one end of the line he wrote the letter A, and at the other end wrote the letter C. Everything in between A and C was labeled B. "Now you're telling me there's nothing in the twenty-five-mile radius of B!" Though Eugene didn't speak much English, he smiled watching Arley carry on.

Arley was right, but I didn't want to dink around in area B, all day, looking for a fish, when I already knew where there were plenty of fish to be caught. We had this little argument almost every outing. Irene would always side with me, so Arley would be out-voted. After about a forty-five-minute bouncy ride, we were on the spot. I lowered the anchor, and it was time to fish.

Irene quickly baited her hook and down to the bottom she went. I got Eugene set up and gave him a quick lesson on halibut fishing. Pretty simple: put a herring on a hook, nothing fancy, drop your bait to the bottom, put your pole in the pole holder, and sit back and wait for a stupid halibut to bite. Halibut aren't too smart. Imagine grabbing a bait that is mostly all hook and just chomping down so hard it drives the hook right through your head. Dumb-ass fish.

Arley finally finished massaging his bait and away it went, down, down, down to about twenty feet. Arley was not interested in reeling in a halibut these days. As soon as Arley went into the cabin, I dropped his line another two hundred feet to the bottom.

It wasn't long, and Eugene and I joined Arley in the nice warm cabin for doughnuts and coffee. We three wussy guys watched the poles from inside the warm cabin, while Irene manned the deck. It was a cold, rainy, ugly day, but Irene didn't mind—she had dressed warmly and had full rain gear on. It didn't matter how nasty the weather and seas were, Irene would always smile and say, "It's not that bad out here." A little rain and wind wasn't going to change the way she liked to fish. She had to be holding and slowly rocking her pole up and down, enticing a bite. As far as she was concerned, it was a great day to be fishing.

Occasionally, Eugene would leave the warm cabin and emulate Irene's method of rocking the rod. After about five minutes in the wind and cold he would retreat and join the two pansies in the cabin. If it were up to Arley, he would still be in his nice warm bed. Arley enjoyed his sleep more and more each year. If it weren't for Irene's love for fishing, Arley would spend most of his days on land.

After about an hour, we began getting bites and catching small halibut. Eugene had a ball. Not only was he catching fish on his rod, he was taking care of Arley's too. "I didn't let my line to the bottom, and I'm not reeling it all the way back in," Arley whined. "Eugene," he yelled, "when you get that one in, there's one on my rod too." I was releasing small halibut as fast as Eugene could get them to the surface.

I began putting bigger baits on in hopes of catching a bigger fish. We'd caught some gray cod and turbot earlier, and I began using them as bait in addition to the herring. I put large pieces of cod on a couple of rods, and a half a turbot, head and all, on Irene's rod. If something grabbed that, it would have to be a bigger fish.

The bigger baits slowed the action way down. The three wussies continued to fish from inside the cabin. Arley had me laughing as usual with his great stories. I never got tired of listening to Arley's stories. Some stories became even more entertaining after the third or fourth time. Eugene didn't understand much of what Arley was saying, but he could tell it was funny and he laughed along with me. The three cabin boys were having such a good time socializing in the cabin, we had nearly forgotten about the loan fisherwoman on the back deck.

Suddenly, I heard a faint voice crying for help from out on the deck. I looked out and could see Irene slumped over the side of the boat. Irene had hooked something huge, and it was all but dragging her into the water. I ran out and began helping Irene get control of whatever she had on. The monster was running toward the bow and had Irene keeled over the side, trying to avoid being dragged to the bow herself.

"Dan, take the pole. I'm going to lose it." I grabbed the rod, and Arley put the fighting belt on Irene.

Arley hollered, "Woman, what in the hell are you doing out here!"

There was no doubt Irene had a lunker on. She had her reel set on full drag, and it wasn't slowing the brute down a bit. I guided the rod into the fighting belt for her. Irene hung on for dear life, while the line continued to peel off the reel. "Dan, Dan, my line!" she squealed. I looked at her reel and could see the final knot at the end of the line. I cranked her drag down as hard as I could and put two thumbs on the last of the line, and slowly the line stopped.

Irene began slowly coaxing the fish back toward the boat. We were in about two hundred twenty-five feet of water, but the fish had taken over six hundred yards of line. After twenty minutes, Irene had

BIG, BIG FISH!

managed to get a good bunch of line back. It started to look like we might have a chance of landing this thing. The fish made numerous long runs, but then stopped, and Irene worked the big something toward the boat again. I really wasn't sure Irene had a halibut on the end of her line. Usually a big halibut will make a few good runs and then you can slowly work them in. In the back of my mind, I thought she might be hooked up with a four- or five-hundred-pound salmon shark that occasionally fed in the area.

After an hour, Irene had the fish straight up and down. Now came the true test—actually lifting the brute toward the surface. Irene had been playing the fish while it ran around on the bottom, but now it was time for the work of slowly lifting and maneuvering the monster to the surface.

Irene would lift on her rod and the line would just slip out of the reel. The drag could not handle the sheer weight of the fish. The only way to move the brute was to plant a thumb on the line on the face of the reel and lift ever so slowly, and then drop the tip of the rod while reeling in the little bit of slack she had gained. Then she would have to lock her thumb back on the reel so the line couldn't slip.

Irene was exhausted. For the first time ever, she needed help. She had to be whipped if she was asking her husband, Mr. Finesse, to take a turn. If the fish was ever going to get away, I was sure it would be soon. Arley took one lift on the rod and looked at me. "There's no fish on here; we've snagged bottom!" About then, the fish took back everything Irene had gained. Arley gave me another look. "This ain't no halibut!"

I wasn't so sure it was a halibut either, but I sure wanted to see what was on the other end of the line. It had to be a huge halibut or a big shark.

Arley worked on the beast for about fifteen minutes and he was shot. He was in his late eighties now, and his back had really become a problem for him. He tried not to show it, but he was living in a lot of pain. Lifting a Volkswagen two hundred feet under the water probably wasn't the treatment he needed.

It was time for Eugene to take a turn. We strapped him into the fighting belt. Eugene's facial expression showed his shock at the weight of the fish. He lifted on the rod and his eyes grew bigger. All he could say was, "Oh, oh, big fish! Big, big fish!" Five minutes later, he shook his head side to side. He was done.

Arley and Eugene had given Irene a short rest, but that was all she was going to get. Again, Arley got the belt on Irene, and I maneuvered the rod into place for her. Irene was in control again. She slowly began lifting the lunker to the top. She had her thumb on the reel as she lifted the rod and reeled fast on the way back down to pick up the slack that she had gained. Slowly but surely the mammoth was being worked to the surface.

I could see a mark at about one hundred feet on the sounder (fish finder). The mark was Irene's fish—she was almost to the halfway point! "Young man," Arley spouted, "if you ever want to see this boat go home, you are going to have to put on that belt and take over!" I began helping Irene lift up on the rod each time and then she would drop the rod and reel in the slack she had gained. She was absolutely exhausted, but with her adrenaline and a little extra lifting power, we were making good progress now. Thumb on reel, both of us lifted, reel down. Arley was on sounder watch; he would yell out the depth of the fish. "Seventy-five feet, sixty-five feet!" We were not far from seeing what was on the end of Irene's rod. "Twenty-five feet," Arley called out. "He's got to be right there!"

Slowly a large dark shadow began to appear. It was a monster-sized halibut! Arley took a look at it, "My God man! Look at the size of that thing!"

Eugene ran around as if his head was cut off, saying, "Big fish! Big, big fish!"

After two hours of battling, we could finally see what was on the end of Irene's line. "Well, Arley," I said, "Irene has caught it. Now shall we let it go?"

Arley looked at me. "Are you out of your mind, man? Irene will never catch a fish like this again. We have to get him in the boat. This is a fish of a lifetime!" How soon he had forgotten about never wanting to catch a big halibut. Maybe just one more.

I had a long line with a shark hook tied to the end. I don't like using a harpoon. "Okay," I said, "Irene, slowly bring the brute to the surface just so I can grab the leader." The leader was made of an eight-hundred-pound test ganion (heavy leader material), so there were no worries about it breaking.

Irene brought the fish up slowly, and I grabbed the leader. The halibut had her mouth wide open. I rammed the shark hook into the upper part of the fish's mouth. She lay there just long enough so I could slam her between the eyes with my trusty aluminum bat.

I continued pulling up on the shark hook line and pounding the fish in the head. I threaded a heavy line through the gills and jaw and tied the halibut off to a cleat on the side of the boat. Then I tied a loop around the tail and secured that line to the stern cleat. We had the big soaker now. I got the biggest hug from Irene; she was so happy.

"Now *that's* a fish!" Arley said. "Just look at that thing!"

Eugene was still babbling in broken English, "Big fish, big fish!"

I cut the halibut's throat, and we let it bleed and jerk against the lines. Even though she'd been bashed in the head forty times and had her throat cut, she continued jerking around alongside the boat for a while.

Eugene fished for another fifteen minutes while we waited for the big girl to bleed out and settle down. Sure enough, Eugene hooked a fish just before we pulled his line in for the day. It was nothing like Irene's, but a forty-pound halibut was by far the biggest fish he had ever caught.

I kept looking at Irene's fish alongside the boat. "Why do you keep looking at that fish?" Arley asked.

"Well, I am trying to figure out how we are going to get the damn thing in the boat." I had my doubts that I had enough manpower to break the fish over the side and into the boat. Arley assured me we could do it. I let the tail end go on the fish. Then Irene and Eugene pulled on one line, Arley pulled on the line connected to the shark hook, and I pulled on the gaff hook I had sunken into the halibut's head. We all pulled for all we were worth and didn't come close to breaking the fish over the side. I re-secured the halibut to the side of the boat. It was time for plan B. I had a snatch block on the boat. I attached it to the overhang of the roof on the opposite side. Then I threaded the line connected to the halibut through the block. I had Arley, Irene, and Eugene pull down on the line, and I pulled up on the brute with a gaff. Each time they pulled down and I pulled up, the fish creeped up the side. On about the fifth pull, over the side she came.

Arley could finally relax. He wasn't counting that fish as caught until he actually saw it in the boat. It was only noon, but it felt much later. Up came the anchor and we bounced our way back to town. When we got to town I brought the boat to the South Harbor to the fish-hanging station.

After tying the boat up, I got some extra manpower and we got the brute out of the boat. We winched her up and got pictures with the Haeners and Irene's monster-sized halibut. The big butt was estimated at around 370 pounds. Beautiful, white-haired Irene had her halibut of a lifetime. It wasn't long before word had gotten out about the big fish on the dock. Soon after, the newspaper reporter was interviewing the Haeners. I heard Arley say something like, "Hell, I've been passed by smaller cars than that thing!"

I told Arley, "If Irene's fish would have been a pound bigger, I would have cut the line. Nobody's going to break my record of 371 pounds on my boat"! I just smiled.

Irene, Arley, and me.

Until We Meet Again

THE FISHING TRIPS with the Haeners became fewer and fewer. Irene would fish every day if she could, but Arley's back and joints were causing him severe pain. He would still go fishing if the seas were calm, just for Irene. They were a package, and Irene and Arley almost always went fishing together.

Irene had talked Arley into joining a charter I had scheduled in the morning. The weather was going to be good, and Arley was feeling okay that night. Irene was so excited; she hadn't been fishing for over a week. Irene had a routine of getting up early, going for her morning walk, stopping by for coffee at our house, then walking back to their bed and breakfast. Arley would usually still be sleeping when she returned. He'd always say that there was no pain when he slept.

The next morning, I went by the Stockton's bed and breakfast to pick up Arley and Irene to go fishing. I walked in very quietly like I always did, poured a cup of coffee, and sat down in the chair in the living room. Irene soon came walking in, already dressed and anxious to go fishing. She looked great as usual—not a hair out of place and no makeup. She was beautiful. Most women look like two different people in one body. There's your morning woman (which can be a bit frightening before her first trip to the "put a little makeup on" room), and then there's the new woman who emerges after a little tidying up and a cup of coffee. Cheryl and Irene are the exceptions. They wake up looking beautiful every day.

Irene joined me and we slowly drank our coffee, while we waited for Arley. When Arley came into the living room, he was not dressed to go fishing. He hadn't slept most of the night because of his back. "Irene," he said, "I'm so sorry, but I'm in too much pain to go today. I need to stay and try to get some sleep. Dan, you take Irene and I'll try to sleep this day away."

Irene wanted no part of it. They came as a package, and she wasn't going to leave Arley. Arley looked at Irene and said, "Irene, my fishing days are over. I've caught all the fish I want to catch in my life. You still love to fish. Now go with Dan and catch a great big one. Have a great day, and I'll be rested when you get back."

Irene wanted to go so badly, so she reluctantly said, "Okay, Arley, I'll go." She gave Arley a big hug, and I reassured her that everything would be fine. Irene and I headed to the harbor and met up with the two men patiently awaiting our arrival.

I introduced the men to Irene, and all aboard, and off to the fishing grounds we went. It was the first time Irene went solo. It seemed like a much longer boat ride without Arley telling his stories and poking fun at me. We loved poking fun at each other. "You have *no idea*," he'd always say to me.

It started out as a normal halibut charter, but I quickly noticed that Irene wasn't herself today. I quickly baited the guys' lines and gave them a lesson on dropping to the bottom and being patient when fish started biting. "Let it hook itself. Don't try to set the hook; these are a different breed of fish," I'd say. "They are stupid fish."

Soon, the two men had their lines on the bottom and were fishing. Irene was still sitting in her chair. She was always the first one baited and first to the bottom, but not this morning. Her right-hand man was not here, and Irene was somewhere else. She was thinking about Arley, not about fishing. I baited her up and she began letting her line down. Again, I reassured her that Arley would be fine, that he was happy she was fishing today, and that she should try to have fun and enjoy herself.

I told the two men they had to put five dollars apiece into the pot for the biggest fish. I bet on Irene, because she always caught the big ones.

I looked over to see how Irene was doing. She was still letting out line! She had hit bottom five minutes ago, and now the current was just taking her line out. I stopped her line and reeled it in until it was sitting on the bottom. This had to be one of the longest days of Irene's life. It soon became evident that Irene could not operate without her partner. She continued to let line out for no reason throughout the day. Then I would get her back on the bottom and she would start reeling in her line. I felt terrible. I would have loved to have called it a day and gotten her back to Arley, but I couldn't cut the charter short.

By the end of the day, the two men had caught some nice halibut. It was time to bring the lines in and head back to town. The guys brought their lines in, and I got Irene to begin reeling in. She had the better half of her line out again. As she brought her line in, her rod took a slow jerk.

Could you believe it? Irene had hooked a big halibut. Irene didn't play the fish with her normal smooth expertise, but she got the fish to the boat. It was a nice, eighty-pound halibut. The biggest fish of the day. Irene had won the pot. An hour later, we were back to town. Irene gave her fish to the two men. She just wanted to get home to Arley. It had been a crazy day. Irene had completely forgotten how to fish. She just couldn't function without her partner.

Before we walked through the door of the bed and breakfast, Irene gave me the biggest, longest hug she'd ever given me. "Thanks for a wonderful day," she said. "Now you have to promise me something. You can never tell Arley about today."

I just said, "What are you talking about? It was a great day. You caught the biggest fish and took my clients' money."

Irene never went fishing without Arley again. Over the next couple of summers, she started showing signs of Alzheimer's. Fishing trips became few and far between. Arley continued to live with extreme aches and pains, and soon their summers in Petersburg came to an end. Irene passed away on June 23, 2007, at the age of eighty-eight. Arley could not live without Irene and joined her on January 19, 2009, at the age of ninety-three. It was a great day when that old fart told me I was going to teach him how to fish, and I will never forget the wonderful memories made with our dear friends, the Haeners. Goodbye, beautiful Irene and Arley. Love you always. Until we meet again.

Great couple

First King Crab Season

IN 2004, I took an early out, with a retirement incentive package, from Alaska Airlines. The same spring, Cheryl and I also sold Northern Lights Smokeries, the small smoked salmon and seafood processing business we had been running for the past ten years. We made a lot of big life changes in just a few months. That included buying a new house, since our previous house sat on the same property as the business and was sold as part of the package deal. I was only forty-nine years old and would not be eligible for a monthly retirement check until I reached fifty-five. All I had now was my charter business in the summer. I knew what money we had managed to save would not last long, so I needed a winter job.

My brother, Dennis, needed a deckhand on the F/V *Banter Bay* for the 2004 tanner and king crab season, starting in mid-February. I had fished with Dennis off and on, usually filling in crabbing for Dungeness and long-lining for halibut and cod. But that was back in the eighties (damn I'm old!). This tanner and king crab gig was totally new to me, but I was game and was hoping it would work out to an annual winter job.

I would be crewing with Mike Hamer and Dennis's daughter, Holli...all 108 pounds of her, soaking wet. She was not big, but she'd grown up commercial fishing with her dad, and she was an excellent fisherwoman. Mike was an experienced hand, and I valued the knowledge from my fellow deckhands. We fished tanners for three or four days, and then reconfigured the escape rings (openings in the pots that enabled the small crab to get out) on the pots and moved them to king crab grounds.

Once we had all one hundred pots set for king crab, Holli was done and it was just Mike and me on deck. The workload goes way down once the pots are all in the water. Thank God, we had Holli to do the tanner season with us. If it were up to her, she would have stayed through the king season, but heavy shots of line and four hundred- to six-hundred-pound pots take their toll on a large man, not to mention a small woman. I'm sure Dennis made that decision for her.

We left port on February 14, 2004. It was a cold winter day with a temperature around twenty degrees. Add a twenty-five to thirty-five mph wind, and it brought the wind chill down to around zero degrees. We were headed to a bay where we had all our pots stored on some sheer rocks.

We arrived that night and began loading and recottoning each pot as it was hoisted aboard with our hydraulics. Every pot has a strip of cotton threaded in the web. It lasts for about thirty days and then rots out to give all crab or other trapped sea life a way to get out of the pot. Pots get lost, break off, or sink, because they don't have enough line on them. Without a cotton strip, everything would die in the pot, and then more critters would come to feed on the dead and the cycle would continue—meaning a pot without a cotton would cause a lot of unnecessary death.

The next morning, we began filling bait cans and baiting pots. At noon, the season officially opened, and we began setting out pots as fast as possible. I was the "master baiter" and spent the day baiting pots, moving buoy line, and learning from my counterparts. If I wasn't doing something, Holli or Mike would give me something to do in a hurry! I learned on the run. The nice thing (one of the only nice things about tanner fishing) is that you mainly fish in protected areas in bays where the weather is much nicer than being in the open waters, which is where we would be fishing for king crab after we finished with tanner fishing.

After setting our eighty pots, we took a well-needed three-hour nap. I don't know about Holli and Mike, but this *old*, new deckhand was shot! I soon learned that set day was a bitch, with a capital B! Run, run, run, bend over, climb up in the pot to bait it, climb back down the pot. Holy shit, I was going to have to earn every dime.

We began hauling our pots at around midnight. It was extremely exciting for about the first five pots. Pot up, pot to the launcher, pull the pucker line (this lets the crab out), pot back up in the air, and all the crab fall to the deck. Sixty to one hundred or more crab in a single pot! Now the crab had to be sorted and measured. All the legal-sized crab were tossed into the giant fish hold, and the undersized crab went back over the side. Holli and Mike got the pot baited and back in the water, and I began measuring crab. After the pot was launched back into the water, Holli and Mike joined in the sorting before we got to the next pot, which was only about five minutes away. Again, we repeated the process, one person running the valve for the hauling block, one person coiling the line as the pot was being retrieved, and the third wheel (me) finished up sorting crab from the previous pot and got some cans baited for the next pot. Hot damn, you talk about fun! By the tenth pot, I had figured out a new system. When I got on all fours, chasing and measuring crab, I just stayed down on my hands and knees until I was done. Then I'd crawl on all fours over to the railing to pull myself up. I was turning into the Hunchback of Notre Dame. I didn't think I'd ever be able to walk normally again.

Holli and Mike felt it too, but nothing like the old goat on the boat! I was soon running hydraulics, tying knots, coiling, and setting pots. There was no doubt a third person was a huge help in tanner fishing.

After three long days of tanner fishing, we began reconfiguring the escape rings in the pots for king crab. After stacking a load of pots on board, we headed out to the open water to set our pots for king crab. Another round of set day, but this time in nasty, rough water. We took three separate loads of pots out to the grounds. The tanner to king crab switch-over was brutal! Hauling gear in rough weather was not fun but very manageable. Setting pots in big seas was extremely hard and very dangerous.

Most vessels in the Southeast Alaska tanner and king crab fishery do not have cranes on board. The boats are not as large as on those on the television show, *The Deadliest Catch*, and a crane would take up too much usable space. We were on a fifty-eight-foot boat compared to the boats over one hundred feet seen on *The Deadliest Catch*. On smaller boats like ours, the pots are lifted and moved to the launcher on spectra lines driven by hydraulics. When the seas get ugly, the pots can easily get out of control when moving from a high stack down to the pot launcher. From the top house, Dennis relayed orders over the loud speaker. Looking out the window from his nice warm wheelhouse window, he was able to see when a set of smaller waves were coming and then give the go ahead to lower a pot off the stack down to the launcher. Communication was huge. If a set of huge waves got close, we could hear the command, "Wait," over the hailer (deck speaker). After the waves passed, the command "Okay," could be heard and the next six-hundred-pound pot descended toward the launcher. Many times, getting a pot to the launcher was not an option. If another set of waves hit while the big pot was still in midair, swinging uncontrollably, it was just lowered as quickly as possible to anyplace on the deck. Any landing was a good landing. Just get it out of the air!

Everyone is always on their toes when setting pots on nasty days. Big, heavy pots dangling off lines can get pretty exciting, to say the least. When working in these conditions you never want to get between a pot and the side of the boat, another pot, the launcher, or really anything that the pot can squish you against when it is swinging on a couple of lines. Always have an exit to get out of the way. When push comes to shove, the pot will win and it could be the end of a season for a crew member, or even worse, the end of a life.

After two rough, ugly, sleepless days of setting one hundred pots, we headed to town to sell our tanner crab. We needed to get them off the boat before hauling our king crab pots. After off-loading our crab, we refueled, got a little more grub, and took a well-deserved rest. One night in town, a home-cooked meal, and a wonderful evening with my beautiful wife was a good respite.

The next morning at 4:00 a.m., Cheryl drove me to the boat. I'll be honest. I did not want to get back on that damn boat. I would rather have gone to the dentist and had my wisdom teeth pulled. I gave Cheryl a big hug and kiss and began my slow, long, walk down the dock to the Banter Bay. I felt like I'd been found guilty as charged. Off to the penitentiary, I was going, and no one was going to post bail. I was going to serve a long, hard sentence on the F/V *Banter Bay*.

It was just Mike and me this time, with Dennis at the helm. Holli had been a huge help tanner fishing and making the switchover to king crabbing.

We left port early in the morning on a beautiful blue-sky day—crystal clear and ten degrees with a cold, northerly wind blowing. The forecast was calling for clear skies, cold temperatures, winds at forty knots, and up to sixty knots out of interior passes. I'd made my choice to take an early out from Alaska Airlines, and I was really not too happy with my decision-making process right now. I was seriously doubting my new chosen profession.

Six hours later, we had arrived at our first pot. It was a challenge just getting the buoy set up into the crab block with the rough sea conditions. We were both dressed in multiple layers to ward off the extreme cold. Mike and I switched back and forth from running hydraulics to coiling the line as each pot was hauled. The hydro man ran the controls to bring the pot up and then to the launcher. Basically, he would be standing and not moving, just freezing his ass off, while the coiler man was throwing line in coils, moving, and keeping semi-warm. We always knew whose turn it was to coil and looked forward to the task that kept the blood flowing.

The pace had slowed from tanner crabbing, and we were on more of a schedule. The king crab don't get in the pots nearly as fast as the tanners, and generally the pots are much deeper. The average pot is anywhere from sixty-six fathoms to three hundred fathoms (each fathom is six feet). In some areas, four hundred fathoms and deeper are the norm. Hauling pots at these depths made for much slower hauling. Instead of hauling eighty to one hundred twenty pots per day tanner fishing, we would only haul thirty to seventy pots a day for the king crab.

With the ugly weather, we were not hauling as many pot as we wanted to. But we were catching enough crab to make it worth our while. Everything just slows down when you're battling the rough seas and frigid temperatures. Changing shots of lines out for different depths takes more time when all the line is iced over and frozen like a brick. Knots get stubborn when frozen, and we were wearing heavier gloves than normal, making untying and retying a knot a bit cumbersome. The good news was, I'd made it through the most painful week of aches and pains that I could ever remember. I'd wrestled in high school and college, and I thought my body had seen the worst. I was wrong, wrong, wrong. Being almost fifty years old didn't help either. My body gets a hell of a lot more sore now than it did when I was in my twenties, and the recovery time is extremely slow.

The northerly continued for a week, and the forecast was calling for more of the same. Most of the boats went back to town to wait it out, but there were a few that just kept fishing and grinding away as long as it was workable. We had to stop at times and go inside for a quick fifteen minutes to have a cup of coffee and warm up a little.

FIRST KING CRAB SEASON

Glazed crab pots

Breaking ice ......

FIRST KING CRAB SEASON

Frozen rails and rigging from freezing spray

After about ten to twelve days of fishing torture, we went into Juneau, Wrangell, or Petersburg—whichever was paying the top dollar for king crab—and get fuel. Then back out we went. We wanted to catch as much of the total quota (amount of crab allotted in an area) as we could. There are different quotas in different areas, and once the quota was caught in an area, all the pots must be moved out of that area. The longer the weather persisted, the more of the quota we were going to catch. The majority of the other boats were not going to battle the conditions, but we were, and it was paying off. We continued to grind away, sometimes not seeing another boat for a week at a time. They don't call my brother a grinder for nothing. He is the ultimate grinder.

Pot full of king crab.

FIRST KING CRAB SEASON

A full hold...Good payday!

We were getting occasional snow squalls, and sometimes we would wake up to five to eight inches on top of the ice-glazed deck. As soon as we poked our noses back out into the weather, the waves would wash all the white away. Our biggest problem was trying to keep the ice from building up on the boat. We were continuously beating ice off with bats and a mallet. Ice gets heavy, and a top-heavy vessel is very unstable. Freezing spray can build ice extremely fast. Our boat was beginning to look like a ghost ship with all the ice hanging from her.

There were a few days we were hauling in weather that made safety a definite concern. Mike and I wore life vests over our rain gear. It actually wasn't that cumbersome, and it gave a feeling of safety, not to mention that it helped keep you warm.

It was on one of the worst days of the year, when a truly surreal thing happened. I was on hydros, and Mike was coiling. I was a bit stressed and nervous with the sea conditions and freezing spray. I looked at the back rail, and there sat this crusty old seagull, and beside him sat the most beautiful white seagull. I automatically thought, *These are my old pals Arley and his beautiful wife, Irene. They were out here looking after us.* I'm not much of a church-goer, but this really gave me a sense of comfort. Throughout the bitter winter king crab season, my old friends made many visits just to make sure we were safe. On nasty days, I always kept my eye out for the Haeners, and still do today.

Keeping us safe

FIRST KING CRAB SEASON

This cold winter season was hard on the seagulls and stormy petrels. The petrels would crash land onto our deck at night. They would be blinded by our crab lights (large sodium lights) and end up on the deck. Some mornings, we would have twenty, even thirty petrels hiding around on the deck. They could not fly off the deck; they needed a lift or throw to catch a little air and fly off. The poor birds would not last long before a flock of seagulls would snatch them out of the air and eat them. This is not the seagulls' normal diet, but they were extremely hungry in this cold winter. If you ever watch a seagull fly, they always have their legs and feet dangling outside their feathers, but not this winter. They had their legs and feet tucked into their feathers and would only bring them out to land. When they landed on the boat, they stood on one leg with the other tucked into their feathers, switching legs to get the other one warm occasionally.

Mike would throw some bait in the air on one side of the boat, and all the seagulls would swarm around him. While the seagulls were distracted, I would throw a stormy petrel off the other side. The little guy would get a good flying start, but soon the gulls would see him and chase him down. Everything was hungry from fighting the cold, including Mike and me. We were burning some serious calories. We both had lost our winter fat. I weighed in at a whopping 145 pounds. I hadn't seen that weight since high school! Mike and I had gotten in pretty good condition. We started doing push-ups and sit-ups between pots to keep warm. I was up to sets of fifty push-ups and sixty sit-ups, and my old body was feeling pretty good.

Our deck hose was frozen up, and our bait was so frozen we chopped it with Mike's axe, and then tried to grind it in the bait chopper. Our fresh water system was frozen for a while, but all the rolling around finally broke it free. We were definitely living a bit like barbarians, but we caught our share of crab, and a lot of other boats' shares of the quota. We were making good money.

The brutal month of February finally passed. Now, halfway through March, the weather had finally settled down. The bitter winter had made the quota go at a snail's pace. On normal years, the quota would have been caught long ago. Thankfully, Mike, Dennis, and I, all got along great. I couldn't imagine being stuck on a boat for long periods of time working with a whiner or a hot head. I wouldn't, simple as that. The job is stressful enough without having to worry about someone's attitude.

The days were getting longer, and the weather continued to get nicer. We were definitely on a schedule now. If you've ever seen the movie, *Groundhog Day*, that was us. Same thing, day after day, after day, after day. Get up at first light, get dressed, a couple cups of coffee, bathroom, quick bowl of cereal, out to the deck, rain gear on, grind bait, pull up to the buoy, hydro man, coil pot up to the launcher, dump crab, pot back to launcher, rebait pot, set pot, measure crab, throw in tank, dump old stinking bait cans, rebait cans, pull up to the next buoy, and repeat the process. This was our groundhog day. We'd do that forty to sixty times a day with a little snacking and lunch in between, then dinner, and off to the bunk. You do this for a couple of months, and a person can go dingy. We'd all run out of stories, and now were just repeating the same ones over and over. I gave Mike courtesy nods when he told me the same story for the fifth time, and he'd do the same for me.

Finally, by the first of April, the Fish and Game announced that the area we were in would be closing, and all pots must be out of this area within forty-eight hours. It was a glorious day. The quota had been caught!

It took a day and a half to get our gear pulled and set back on the steep rock bank where they rested until the next season. It took us three loads of pots to get them back to their home. What a wonderful feeling, knowing we were stacking the gear for the last time and then, home sweet home!

At last, all of our pots were again resting on the steep rock embankment, all but five that is. These five pots were in an area where the quota had not yet been met, so there was no hurry to get them out of the water. It was a great feeling to see all of our pots on the rocks as we pulled away to go retrieve the last and final five king crab pots.

Mike and I were all smiles as we pulled up to the first pot. We were on easy street now. Final countdown…get these last five in, put them on the rocks, and take this vessel to town! Home again, home again, it never sounded so good! The first pot came up, and it had a few crab in it. On board it came. We pulled the second one, and it had a few crab in it too. On board it came. Only three more pots to go. Up came the third pot, and it had more crab than we anticipated in it. Mike and I could hear Captain Brother Dennis talking to himself. "Wow, isn't that interesting?"

Mike looked at me and said, "You don't think…he wouldn't, he couldn't. Would he?" The fourth pot had a few more crab in it. Mike and I had lost our smiles. We looked up in the wheelhouse watching Dennis scratching his head. We both thought the exact same thing. Holy shit, this final pot of the season had better be a big fucking zero! We both knew by the look on Dennis's face that if we had even one crab, we would be setting all our pots back in the water. There was still quota to catch in this area. Up came our final pot.

It was like a nightmare! Three crab! Captain Brother Dennis slowly walked out of the wheelhouse and looked down at us. He looked just like Jack Nicholson in *The Shining*! "Here's Johnny!" He knew he was not going to be very popular when he told us we were going to reset all the gear, but he saw a chance to make a nice chunk of change. That's what makes him an excellent fisherman.

The two of us were in a bit of shock, but we knew if it paid off, it would all be worth it in the end. I would just have to spend another week or two on my prison sentence. Back to the rocks we went, to get more pots.

It was setting day all over again. It was fucking *Nightmare on Elm Street*! At least this time, my body was a bit more conditioned, and I wouldn't have to go through nearly the healing process from the aches and pains that I'd gone through on the first go-around back in February.

After fishing for another week, we had pretty much mopped up what was there. It wasn't what we'd hoped for, but it was more money in all of our pockets. This time, the pots came out of the water and onto the rocks to stay. You never know unless you roll the dice. It had been a hard, long crab season and a very successful one. The Grinder made it happen!

After we were all finished, and back in Petersburg, Captain Dennis asked Mike and me if we were on for next year. We both smiled. I said, "Can you ask us that question in a month? I need to forget parts of this season first."

We both said yes, we would go again next year. And we did. In fact, five years later, I'm still king crabbing, at age fifty-four, with my brother. I'm definitely the old goat on the boat. I try to get in fairly good shape before each season, so I can survive the first few days of setting and moving pots. I don't know how many years I've got left in me. It's definitely a season-to-season call. The guy at the pointy end of the boat will definitely outlast the old guy on the blunt end. I wear lots of clothes and rain gear. He wears slippers, jeans, and a shirt. I'll stay in the guiding business in the summers, and hopefully continue doing some commercial pot shrimping with Dennis and his youngest daughter, Megan, in the winter. Shrimping involves light pots, lots of fun, and is much easier on an old man.

Author with giant king crab

Doubleheader

IT WAS 5:30 a.m., and I had my four trolling rods baited and in the water. When I'm not chartering or commercial fishing with my brother, I'm usually commercial hand trolling for king salmon or cohos on my own boat. I have two choices of gear when hand trolling. I can use hand gurdies spooled with heavy wire and run multiple different hoochies, bait, or spoons off of them. Or I can use four salmon rods. I'll use gurdies for cohos but do better using four fishing rods for kings. Plus, there's nothing like fighting a king salmon on a limber rod.

After about an hour of trolling, I had a hookup on one of my four rods. I began fighting the king and clearing the other rods out of the way to prevent a tangle. One guy and four rods can be tricky at times. I finally maneuvered the thirty-pound fish to the boat. As I attempted to slip the net under the king, he outmaneuvered me. Just as I went to scoop the nice fish, he made a quick turn to avoid the net, and I ended up getting the hooks caught in the net, with the fish still attached on the outside of the net. I made a snap decision to just let go of the net before the fish broke the leader. Now I had a king salmon and a net on my line.

I fought the fish and net for about ten minutes until the king was exhausted from pulling my net around. I finally maneuvered the tangled mess to the boat and was able to grab the net and spin it under the fish. I'd gotten away with a major mistake. The fish gods were with me today for sure.

By noon, I had two more kings that were about fifteen pounds each. Then the fishing went dead. I had planned on spending the night on the boat but was having second thoughts. By 6:00 p.m., still no more action... six hours without a bite. I talked myself into going home to a nice warm bed and a nice warm wife. I had just enough time to pull my lines in and get to town before it was dark.

Just as I was going to grab the first rod to reel it in, *shwack-o!* The rod tip jerked down, and line began pulling off the reel. I grabbed the rod out of the holder and *ka-slamo*...my stern rod went down, and I was hooked up with a second fish. Six hours without a strike, and just like that, I had a doubleheader on.

I left the fish on the stern rod in the holder and worked on clearing the other two rods while playing the first fish. The fish I was working on, felt like a big one. So I was really being careful not to break the line. In fact, I paid so much attention to the fish I was playing, I hadn't realized I was running out of line on the stern rod. When I looked back, I could see I was about to lose everything on the unmanned pole! I was about to be spooled. In a panic, I jammed the rod I was working in a holder and made a mad dash for the stern rod. It was too late! The line was flying off the reel, and when it came to the end, the whole pole went shooting out of the holder and into the water heading eastbound!

I yelled a few choice words. I put the boat in gear and began making wide circles while I played the other fish. It was a Hail Mary, but I thought maybe I could continue fighting the fish I still had on, and I might be able to run it across the other line and get it back. I was only in thirty feet of water in a fairly narrow area. There was a pole and three hundred yards of line being drug around by a fish down there.

It was now dark, and after a few circles it looked like a lost cause. I pulled my exhausted fish in. I had one more idea. I ran the boat about a quarter mile up the beach in the direction I last saw my pole heading. I then dropped my anchor down twenty-five feet, put the boat in reverse, and began zigzagging back and forth, hoping to intercept the line on my anchor gear. I did this for twenty minutes with no movement on the anchor line.

I yelled a few more choice words and hauled my anchor. I didn't see anything at first, but just as the anchor was going into its bracket, I thought I saw a line. I jumped on the bow to get a better look, and yes, I had my fishing line across my anchor! I brought the line to the back of the boat and began pulling it in by hand. It was just slack, like no resistance at all. I was sure I was going to get a pile of line with nothing on either end.

I continued gathering slack line, and then I felt a little resistance. It felt like about the weight of a fishing pole! I'd written the fish off long ago. I just wanted to get the pole and reel back. Those things aren't cheap. I pulled very slowly and steadily. I didn't want the knot to break or slip off the reel.

Finally, I was there. I gently lifted to get the pole out of the water, and to my surprise it wasn't a fishing pole. It was a huge king. There was no way I was going to just hand-line this fish into my net. One quick run with the line in my hand would result in a snarl and a broken line. I watched the king swim by and disappear into the darkness. I began letting the pile of fishing line back out again, making sure not to make a big snarl. Finally, all the line I had brought in was out again, and I began pulling line toward the other end; hopefully the end that still had my rod connected to it. After a few minutes of retrieving line, I felt a little tension. Carefully, I pulled and there it was. Now I had my pole, and I also had a huge king on the other end of three hundred yards of line!

The king came in much easier this time. He'd been whipped by a fishing pole. Finally, I'd reached the other end of the line, and the exhausted lunker surrendered into the net! Needless to say, it was dark and I was not going home now. I anchored the boat for the night and had a beverage to celebrate my doubleheader. I went to sleep with a big fat smile on my face. The first fish weighed in at thirty-five pounds, and Mr. Big was forty-four pounds. Best doubleheader of my life…so far!

Hall of Famer

IN MAY OF 2010, I got the pleasure to take the Hall of Famer, baseball great, George Brett, fishing for three days. Along with George, I had his brother Jeff, and their good friends, Jack and John, who had set the charter up.

George Brett has always been my baseball hero. I grew up watching him play third base for the Kansas City Royals. I'll never forget the famous game when George hit the big home run and put the Royals on top. It looked as though that would be the blow to win the game, but before the next batter came to the plate, the New York manager had a conference with the home plate umpire, and the next thing you knew, George was being kicked out of the game for using too much pine tar on his bat! The home run became a big fat out. If you've never seen it, you need to Google the internet for the George Brett pine tar incident. To say the least, George was not a happy camper!

I was extremely nervous about the charter. I wanted to catch fish in the worst way. The first morning of the charter started out exactly the way I didn't want it to…no fish. Two hours of trolling for kings, and not a strike. These guys all had great senses of humors, and I was the brunt of most of the jokes. "So Dan, if a fish were to actually hit one of these rods, what would it look like?" I was fishing with jokesters just like myself. They were having a great time just being out on the boat, playing cards, and catching up on old times.

HALL OF FAMER

Two more hours went by and still not a wiggle. The guys were all inside the cabin telling more stories and playing cards. I was out on deck continuously changing flashers, putting new baits on, and trying different depths, but having zero success. George opened up the cabin door and said, "Hey Captain Dan, we were having coffee at The Moose this morning with a bunch of older locals." Trying not to smile he continued, "Well, they said we're in good hands. They assured us that we have the best guide in town. We were just wondering what the worst one would be like!" Ouch. George had my sense of humor. I needed to see a fish hit a line...any size fish. Just give me a reason to call the gang out of the cabin. I wasn't getting paid to take them out on the boat to play cards!

After twenty-five years in the guiding business, I knew that sometimes you just can't make the fish bite. I changed locations but came up empty in those spots too. By early afternoon, I'd moved back to the same spot we had started. Fishing was slow to say the least.

The guys had changed their bets. Instead of $20 for the first fish, it was now $20 for the first bite. Instead of $50 for the biggest fish, it was now $50 for a fish...any fish. George and his brother came out of the cabin and assured me that they had the utmost confidence in me. They wanted to make sure I knew that they were having a great time. All you can do is give it your best shot and if they don't bite, they don't bite.

By midafternoon, the cabin was full and the bullshit was really flowing. I was on the deck thinking to myself, *Those guys are going to The Moose for coffee before we go fishing tomorrow.* The Moose is one of the gossip centers for the whole town. Everyone in a one-hundred-mile radius will know I posted a big zero! Tomorrow morning the word would be out.

Just when I had lost all hope, George's brother's rod went down! There was a God. I opened the door, "Fish on!"

Out they came like a herd of buffalo. Jeff was literally throwing bodies out of his way to get to his rod. John, George, and Jack started clearing the downriggers and the other rods so they wouldn't snarl with Jeff's. Everyone was dodging and weaving and trying to stay out of Jeff's way. They looked like a fine-tuned machine. Actually, it looked more like a Chinese fire drill.

Ten minutes later, we had a twenty-pound king in the net! A few pictures, and into the fish box he went. I'd barely gotten the poles back in the water and *wham!* George's rod took off. Out of the cabin they came. They were much smoother clearing rods and getting the downriggers up this time. A couple of jumps, a couple of nice runs, and into the net the fish came. George had caught his first Alaskan king salmon! It wasn't quite as big as his brother's, but it was a beauty! (Thank you, God.)

I'd gone from zero to hero. I wouldn't have to hold them hostage to keep them from going to The Moose in the morning! We gave it another forty-five minutes, and called it a day. I brought the downriggers in and got the boat ready to head home.

When I got in the cabin, George was at the helm. "Are we ready, Captain Dan?" He fired up the dual 250 Yamahas. "Okay, now which way is home?" I pointed the direction, and away he went. George was driving us home. I helped him with the trim tabs and RPMs. I figured if George hits an iceberg or a log, he could cover a new boat; a really nice big new boat!

On day two, I had done a little scheming of my own. After being the brunt of the jokes the first day, I was going to pull a little joke on George Brett. Before the boys showed up to the boat, I prepared a special bottle of herring oil attractant. It was actually the same old squirt bottle of herring oil, but I put my own unique label on it. The label read *Pine Tar* in big bold letters. I placed the bottle on the corner of the bait table.

Soon the guys showed up, and George drove the boat to the fishing grounds. The guys were very slow moving this morning. The Moose had become their favorite social hang out—cocktails at night and coffee in the morning. The gear was soon in the water, and the cabin boys were drinking coffee and playing cards. This morning started off just like the previous morning…slow, slow,

HALL OF FAMER

and slower.

After two hours of nothing, George yelled out the cabin door, "Hey Captain Dan, I have a great idea! How about tomorrow we just sleep in until the afternoon bite!"

After another hour and no bites, George piped out, "Captain Dan, I asked the cronies at The Moose, if Dan's the best guide, what do you get with the worst guide?"

It was time for my joke! I asked George if he wanted to bait his own herring. "Sure!" he said, "I'll give it a go!" After a couple of minutes and a little guidance, George had his presentation on the hooks.

Now I said, "Grab that bottle of secret sauce and squirt it on your herring, but don't use too much!"

George grabbed the bottle and began squirting the "pine tar" herring oil on his herring. Then he focused on the label. His eyes got huge and his face turned red. "PINE TAR, PINE TAR!" He chased me around the deck. "Why you little son of a bitch!" he said. "A career batting average of over three hundred and a major league baseball Hall of Famer, and I'll always be remembered as the pine tar guy!"

The boat was in hysterics watching George Brett having an absolute hissy fit. "I sure hope you know how to swim!" I must admit, I was a bit nervous. George could dish it out, and lucky for me he could take it too.

It turned out to be a decent day. We caught three nice kings and lost a couple. While George was guiding my boat back to the harbor, he asked, "Where are we eating dinner?" I volunteered our house and they accepted. I probably should have arranged this in the morning or the day before. Cheryl really doesn't like these kinds of surprises. Thank God I wear the pants in the house (when she's not in the house). I got home about 4:30 p.m. and told Cheryl that George and the guys were coming over at 6:00 for dinner. She smiled and said, "Yeah, sure they are."

"Really, I'm not kidding, dear." The next thing I knew I had a vacuum in one hand and a rag in the other. I was wearing the pants, and

I decided the house needed to be cleaned before I cooked dinner.

The guys came over at 6:00 p.m. with multiple bottles of wine. Julie was also there for fresh king salmon and smoked black cod on the BBQ.

Scott was in Bristol Bay commercial gill-netting for sockeye salmon and would have to miss dinner with the Hall of Famer. Scott was still on my shit list. Before he went to the bay, he had stood me up for fishing on the last day of the annual salmon derby. I told Scott the night before it would just be the two of us on the boat. "Be at the boat at 4:00 a.m. If you're a no-show, Dad's gonna be pissed!"

During the evening, I conveyed this story to the group. George was appalled. "Julie," he said, "get me some paper and a pen. I need to write Scott a little letter." After drinking more than his fair share of wine, George composed a letter scolding Scott for standing his dad up. George later signed Scott's catcher's glove. I wish Scott could have been there to meet him.

The black cod and salmon were a real treat for everyone. The guys had the girls giggling at their stories all evening. The wine may have had something to do with that. They left around 10:00 p.m. but didn't go home directly home. The boys had to make sure The Moose was still there.

On day three, I had four tired fishermen. Late nights and early mornings had taken its toll. We managed to put two more kings in the boat on our last day. It was a quite a day—no cards, no stories, no pranks. The only noise coming out of the cabin was snoring. It had been a great three days.

This trip had come to an end, but the memories will never be forgotten...good times, lots of laughs, decent fishing, and great friends. George put on a baseball clinic for the kids while in Petersburg, which was a huge hit. Hopefully he will be back with his friends in the future.

HALL OF FAMER

Good Day, Bad Day

LOU AND CHARLIE have been fishing with me for almost as long as I've had my charter business. They both love Petersburg and continue to come back to fish with me. Charlie's wife, Lou, is truly a die-hard halibut fisherman. Charlie loves to fish, but he'd much rather watch Lou squeal and reel them in. Over the years, Lou and Charlie have become great clients and even closer friends.

On July 3, 2006, Lou, Charlie, and a good friend of theirs, Ted, boarded my boat to go fishing for halibut for the day. It was always a great day when I had this couple on board—fishing and catching up on what had been happening in each other's lives since we'd seen each other last. On this beautiful July day, we were fishing on a small hump in the middle of Frederick Sound. I can't always fish these little pinnacles. The weather has to be nice, and the seas need to be fairly calm, or I can't get my anchor to hold. If the anchor slides sixty feet, we drift into six or seven hundred feet of water in a matter of minutes, which usually makes for an ugly line tangle. Everything was working great today. The anchor hooked on the top of the pinnacle and best of all, the pinnacle had lots of nice halibut on it. Lou's line barely hit the bottom, and she was hooked up with a nice fish. Lou had just started bringing in her fish, and Ted was hooked up too. Poor Charlie hadn't even had a chance to get his line in the water. As soon as Lou and Ted got their fish three-quarters of the way up, I gave Charlie the okay to put his line down. Ted's halibut came up first, a nice forty-pound fish, and right behind Ted's fish came Lou's, a beautiful fifty-pound halibut.

Charlie barely hit bottom and there was a mouth waiting. It looked like Charlie was hooked up with yet another nice halibut. At this rate, it looked like it was going to be a quick day for halibut fishing unless we started catching and releasing and waiting for some bigger fish to fill the limits. This group just wanted to fish for halibut and watch the whales that frequently passed by the boat. Salmon would have to wait for another day. Today Charlie, Lou, and Ted just wanted to fish for big, flat fish on the bottom.

Throughout the day, I must have seen at least eight different boats come by where we were anchored. Some were sport fishermen, but most were larger commercial boats. Some cruised by at a fairly close distance so they could mark my position in their GPS. By doing this, they had a good idea where to set their commercial halibut long lines. After a while it was almost humorous to see a sport boat or commercial boat change course to go see just where the *Julie Kay* was fishing. It felt like my boat was a big magnet, drawing boats to the area. There was no doubt that if a long liner set some gear around this pinnacle, the rewards would be good.

By two o'clock in the afternoon, we were looking for one last halibut to reach our limit. My three elders on the boat had caught and released at least forty halibut, including some very nice-sized fish. Lou and Charlie were in their seventies at the time, and Ted was pushing eighty. They were all tired from catching fish after fish. It was a good kind of tired. This would be a day they would never forget. Charlie hooked the last halibut of the day. I began putting the other rods away and getting the boat ready for the trip home, while Charlie worked on his fish.

Lou brought to my attention that there was another boat heading in our direction to mark the spot. I didn't pay much attention, just another boat coming to check out the area we were fishing. It had become the joke of the day. While I was putting away the last of the fishing gear, I noticed the vessel getting closer to us than he needed to be. I was used to boats passing by pretty close, but he was being plain-ass rude. I went into the cabin and spoke on the radio, "Vessel off Big Creek heading at me. Give me a little room!" The boat was too far off for me to see the name. He did not respond, but the vessel's course changed. It was evident he got the message.

I went back to the deck to help Charlie with the last fish. Lou gave the offending boat a few choice words of her displeasure. We could finally see Charlie's fish…a nice forty-pound halibut to end a great day of fishing. I gaffed him aboard. As I turned around to put the halibut in the fish box, I witnessed my biggest nightmare. The boat I'd radioed was making an extreme change of course. Instead of passing well off my bow, he was now headed right at the side of my boat! Not only was he zeroing in on me, he was moving at about sixteen knots! I was still anchored and unable to get out of his way.

I scrambled to the cabin to start my engines so I could try to move my boat out of his path if at all possible. I put my engines in full reverse, hoping to free my anchor and avoid the collision. It looked like he was going to just miss my bow. Then his big bow shifted to the right. I could not back up! My anchor was holding steady. We were sitting ducks. I could see the white water coming off his bow as he neared impact. I could also see the boat's name, and I screamed it over the radio, "*Pelican, Pelican,* steer hard left. You're going to hit me!" He kept coming. The *Pelican* was destined to run over us. My boat really was a magnet.

I yelled at everyone to lie down on the deck and put out a last second, "Mayday, Mayday, *Julie Kay!*" and shouted out my latitude and longitude position on the radio. I threw life jackets out the door, and then dived onto the deck, just before the F/V *Pelican* made impact. I was sure he was going to cut my boat in two. I had this vision of the F/V *Julie Kay* exploding into flames when the boat made contact. That's what happens in the movies, right? Everyone hung on for dear life as the *Pelican* ran directly over the top of our boat.

How we were still floating, I'll never know. A thirty-eight-foot vessel, traveling at sixteen to eighteen knots, had just hit us at midship and went completely over the top. I looked around and saw everyone was still on deck and the F/V *Pelican* was now on the other side of my boat, still cruising away as if nothing had happened.

We all began yelling and screaming for him to stop. I was sure we were going to sink, and we would need to get on the boat that had just run over the top of us. As we were yelling at the boat to stop, a head poked up from the stern of the boat and looked back at us. The *Pelican* then slowed and turned around, maneuvering his boat within talking distance. "My God," he says, looking at my battered boat, "Did I hit you?" I told him to just stay close while I looked to see how much water we were taking on.

The radio blared away, "*Julie Kay, Julie Kay*, this is the US Coast Guard. Do you copy?"

I ran into my remodeled cabin and radioed them back, "Stand by, I'll get right back to you as soon as I assess the damage."

I could see a fracture in the side of the boat that went from the top of the cabin all the way to the water line. I looked in the bilge area for water, and to my amazement there was very little. I told the man on the F/V *Pelican* that I was going to cut my anchor line, head my boat for shore, and then turn toward town. If I could get the boat up on step, I was sure we could get to town.

I knew the man on the *Pelican*. He was one of the old timers of Petersburg. He was really shaken up. Come to find out, he was all by himself on a commercial halibut trip. He was in the back of his boat, cleaning halibut, while his out-of-date autopilot staggered the *Pelican* all over Frederick Sound until it finally ran over someone.

After cutting my anchor line, I headed the *Julie Kay* for shore. A good friend of mine, Tom Drennan, was in the area and came over to run his boat alongside mine on the trip into town. Tom had heard the mayday call on the radio, followed by a long silence. His first thought was that a whale had breached and landed on my boat.

Lou, Charlie, and Ted were all hunkered together in what was left of the cabin. Ted looked like he might be in shock. He was shaking uncontrollably. Charlie and Lou put a blanket around him and kept a close eye on him on the trip back. Once we were up and running, I informed the Coast Guard of what had happened and gave them all the information they needed.

On the way back, the Coast Guard repeatedly called the F/V *Pelican* on the radio but did not get a response. Finally, as we approached town, the F/V *Pelican* responded to the Coast Guard calls. The conversation went something like this: "*Pelican*, did you hit a vessel in Frederick Sound today?"

"Well yes, I guess I did. I thought I'd hit a log or piece of ice."

"Didn't you see the boat?"

"Yes, I guess I did I see him ten miles away on my radar."

"So, you're saying you never checked or looked for traffic for ten miles?"

"No, I guess I didn't. But I never dreamed he would still be in that area when I got there."

We had been run over by an eighty-four-year-old man who was cleaning halibut in the back of his boat. Basically, he was just letting his boat drive itself. Once back to Petersburg, Ted was checked out by a doctor and was okay, just severely shaken up. My boat was pulled out of the water and definitely finished for the season.

Two days later, I leased another boat, and believe it or not, my first two customers were Lou and Charlie. Ted stayed home. That meant a lot to me because they didn't have to go, but they wanted to.

The owner of the *Pelican* did not come to town the day of the collision. He was so sick about what had happened, he just anchored his boat up for a couple of days. A few days went by, and I had a knock on my door. It was him. The poor guy was unable to talk. He was so ashamed of what had happened. His mistake could have, and should have, killed us. Once he managed to get his emotions under control, we discussed how he could make it right, so I would not be burdened by any of the costs. He informed me that he had no insurance, but whatever the damages were, he was good for them. I gave the man that almost took our lives a hug before he left. He was good to his word and covered all costs.

The eighty-four-year old never fished again and has since passed away. He was a good man who didn't want to let go of what he loved to do. He had just stayed in the game too long. Out of respect for him and his family, I did not mention his name or the real boat name. I will always remember that day as a good day/bad day.

Lou and me with a nice halibut

Surprise

ON AN EARLY August morning, I sat patiently awaiting the arrival of my charter. All I knew about today's charter was that I was taking two women to do some whale watching and possibly a little fishing. For some reason, I was thinking of a couple of ladies in their thirties or forties. I was wrong again. At the top of the ramp, I could see two women slowly moving toward my boat. One was using a cane, and the other one a walker. Nope, they were definitely over forty!

I walked up the dock to greet them and confirm that these were my two ladies for the day. Yes, they were my girls. Jean was in her late seventies and Tina in her early eighties. We exchanged pleasantries on the long, slow walk to the boat. The two ladies had been best friends forever, and they were on their Alaskan dream vacation. The gals were real jokers, always poking fun at one another. They were hilarious, and I could tell we were going to have a very entertaining day.

Loading them on the boat was a real laugh. I don't have a handicap access door on the boat, so we had to figure out a way to get them over the side and into the boat with as little bending of the knees and twisting of the hips as possible.

Jean went on fairly easily. We plopped her on her ass on the side of the boat and then spun her like a top on the side. She was then able to slide her butt off the side and stand up into the boat.

Tina, on the other hand, was not so agile and, being a larger woman, created more of a challenge. I was trying to maneuver Tina from the dock, and Jean was doing her best from inside the boat to help her. We managed to get Tina sitting on the side of the boat with her feet on the dock. Now came the interesting part of trying to lift her legs and spin her on her tush, so her legs were inside the boat. I lifted Tina's legs up and began rotating her counterclockwise into the boat. Though they were short, stubby legs, they were not light. Jean pushed on the back of her right shoulder trying to get her to spin, and giggling the entire time. What are friends for? After some pushing and pulling, we finally spun Tina and plopped her into the boat. Jean and I had just given Tina the ultimate wedge-o-matic. All Tina could say was, "How in the hell am I ever going to get back off this damn boat?"

With my customers safely on board, it was time to go whale watching. We began our excursion heading north in hopes of finding some active whales. It was August, the prime time for whale watching. We traveled along the water at about thirty-five knots, all eyes wide open, looking for spouts.

In the distance, I could see my buddy's boat cruising out to try his luck at some salmon fishing. His boat was very easy to recognize, not necessarily from what it looked like but from how slow it went. I would guess Mel's top speed was about six knots if the tide and wind were pushing him. Within minutes, we passed closely by Mel's boat. We came up on him so fast he didn't see us coming. Mel looked out his side window just in time to see us waving and smiling as we went by him like he was standing still.

Over the radio Mel's voice could be heard, "Good morning, Dan. Looks like you must have found a couple of suckers to go fishing with you. They must not have gotten the memo that you're the worst charter boat operator in Alaska!"

I replied, "Good morning to you and thanks for the vote of confidence." Mel was always the ultimate prankster, and I never missed an opportunity to sneak up from behind his much-slower boat and surprise him as I zoomed by.

We cruised along the beautiful waters of Frederick Sound. It didn't take long before we saw whale spouts in the distance from a pod of seven or eight humpback whales. The laws on viewing the whales are becoming stricter and stricter by the year. There's a fine line between watching the whales and harassing the gentle giants. A mammal that weighs upwards of forty tons deserves its space, so we pulled up at a respectful distance.

Tina and Jean were in awe as they watched the magnificent creatures arch their backs and gracefully dive beneath the surface. We watched this group of whales for about an hour and then moved up the sound to find another pod of whales.

I was looking for a more active group. We saw plenty of whales surfacing and diving but no feeding or breaching like I was hoping for. The girls were happy just seeing flukes and watching and listening to the blows. After another hour with no breaching or bubble net feeding, I asked if they wanted to try a little fishing. Jean was all for trying to catch a halibut. She'd never even seen one, let alone caught one. Tina just wanted to take in the beautiful day and hopefully watch Jean catch her fish. I moved about a half mile and anchored the boat on a shallow pinnacle about one hundred feet deep. It was turning out to be the perfect day. Not only was Jean getting her chance to fish but we were also anchored next to a pod of about fifteen humpback whales. Fishing and whale watching at the same time; this really is a tough job.

Whales

SURPRISE

I soon had Jean baited up and showed her how to let her line to the bottom. This was all new to Jean. "Now Dan, how am I going to know when I have a halibut on the end of this line?"

I joked, "Well, just wrap the line around the end of your pinky. When your pinky flies into the water, you have one on. Then just reel him in." Jean and Tina were starting to get my sick sense of humor.

We were all watching the whales, and almost on cue, Jean's rod took a bend, and line began peeling off her reel. Jean just looked at her pole in disbelief. "Oh my God! Oh my God! What do I do?"

I began giving her instructions. "Just wait 'til the line stops going out and then begin cranking him in."

Soon Jean was reeling her first halibut in. She'd get tired and I'd have her quit reeling and let the pole sit in the holder while she got her energy back. That's the nice thing about halibut fishing…you can take your time bringing them in. Once they're hooked, they're pretty tough to lose.

After a brief rest, Jean was cranking away again and slowly getting her halibut closer to the surface. Tina was all smiles and laughs watching her best friend getting put to the test by a fish.

Finally, it was the moment of truth. We could see Jean's halibut slowly being pulled to the surface. It looked to be about fifty pounds. It was Jean's first and biggest halibut. Jean and Tina had no way of getting the fish home, so they took some pictures of Jean's halibut in the water and I released it.

Poor Jean was pretty well pooped, but she wanted to try for one more. I quickly rebaited her hook and back to the bottom it went. Jean's new bait barely hit the bottom, and she was hooked up again with another fish. Jean, who had still not recovered from landing the first halibut, pleaded with Tina to give her a hand. I just left the pole in its holder, and Tina began slowly cranking on the reel.

Within two minutes Tina was done…finished. Tina was no spring chicken, and I wasn't going to try to encourage her to continue fighting the fish. Tina was not in the best of shape, and the last thing I wanted was to have a medical problem on my boat. I helped her back to her chair so she could catch her breath. Tina gasped, "I'll eat 'em, but I'll be damned if I'm gonna catch 'em!"

Jean quickly took over the rod. This was a much smaller fish, and she was able to bring it in easier than the last one. Jean soon had the fish to the surface, a nice twenty-pound halibut. Jean looked at the fish in the water, "What a shame to come to Alaska and not taste a fresh piece of halibut."

It was a calm day, and we still had a few hours in the trip, so I suggested keeping Jean's halibut and cooking and eating it on the boat while we watched the whales. This idea was a big hit with the ladies. Cook and eat a fish straight out of the water and watch whales at the same time…this really was going to be the true Alaskan experience.

I clubbed Jean's fish between the eyes and cut the fish's throat so it could bleed out. Up came the anchor, and we were off to find another pod of whales to watch while I worked my magic with our freshly caught lunch.

After a twenty-minute run, we drifted alongside about twenty humpbacks. They were a bit more active than what we had encountered earlier in the day. There was lots of tail slapping on the water, waving of pectoral fins, and even an occasional breach. The sounds were incredible—loud groans, grunts, squeals, and the occasional earth-shattering fart sound, and yes, there were some delightful smells too.

While Tina and Jean enjoyed the whales, I began filleting the fish. After filleting and skinning, I cut the fillets into small pieces. Then I mixed up a little beer and McCormick's batter mix in a bowl. I then heated up a pan of hot oil on my trusty cook stove.

My whale watchers had suddenly turned their attention from the whales to the pieces of fish being dipped in the batter and then fried in the hot oil. About thirty seconds in the oil, I started pulling the golden-brown halibut out and onto a plate…yum. I swear these two had drool coming off the sides of their mouths. I continued battering and cooking fish while the already cooked halibut cooled down a little.

Tina couldn't wait any longer, and she grabbed the first piece. Jean was right behind her. The girls looked like my three-year-old grandson eating ice cream—no talking, just eating, and it just kept coming. Jean and Tina were both in agreement that this was by far the best fish they had ever tasted. There really is nothing better than halibut cooked straight out of the water.

We watched whales and ate halibut for the better part of an hour and then headed back toward Petersburg. On our way to town, we could see my buddy, Mel, steaming toward town at about three knots. Tina and Jean got such a kick out of buzzing by Mel earlier that morning, and we decided to give him another surprise.

I came straight up behind him at about thirty-five knots, then banked left so we could pass him on the side he was steering from. The plan was good and had always worked in the past. But not this afternoon.

Mr. Mel saw us coming up from behind, and he had a real surprise for my senior citizens and me. Just as I was coming up the side of the F/V *Misty Maid*, Mel dashed out of his cabin, turned with his hiney toward us, dropped his drawers, bent over, and gave my gals and me a perfect shot of his seventy-year-old white ass!

Tina looked at me in disbelief. "Dan, I need to get that man's number. What a fine looking hiney!" We laughed the rest of the way to town. Mel had given us a real surprise.

It had been a day Jean and Tina would not forget—their true Alaska experience. They'd fished, eaten halibut they had caught themselves, watched more whales than they could have ever imagined, and ended the day with a stranger showing off his bare hiney.

DROPPING MY LINES

Mr. Fair-Weather

IT ALWAYS MAKES for an interesting charter when you get a fair-weather fisherman and the weather just isn't fair. On this early morning in May, I had two long-time friends from Seattle, Washington, going fishing with me. Over the years, Jake and Phil had fished with me many times together and had become close friends. On this fishing adventure, they had brought along one of their good buddies. His name was Doug. Doug was completely new to the fishing game. His biggest fishing adventure was fishing off a dock on a little lake using a piece of corn for bait. Doug fit the bill. He was definitely a fair-weather fisherman. Now he was going fishing with Jake and Phil on a really big lake called Frederick Sound, and there would be no docks in sight.

We headed northbound to try our luck at halibut fishing. The weather was cool, windy, and wet. The water was bumpy, but the three-foot waves were on our stern, so the ride was not bad. Within the hour, I was dropping the anchor so we could start fishing for halibut. The guys soon had their hooks baited with fresh herring and salmon bellies. Down to the bottom the baits went, and the wait for the first bite began. The weather continued to be cool, wet, and windy, and the boat slowly pitched back and forth, side to side. It was very fishable, but the sea conditions were perfect for someone to get seasick.

Jake and Phil were out on the deck, jigging their rods up and down as they laughed about old fishing memories. Doug left his pole in its holder and watched from inside the warm cabin. He was not feeling 100 percent. I tried to get him to focus on land and drink some ginger ale, but it was to no avail. Doug was seasick and was soon chumming for Jake and Phil. "That a boy, Doug, that'll get 'em biting," chirped Jake. Doug staggered back inside to the warmth of the cabin. I kept Doug company inside while we watched Phil and crazy Jake laughing and having a great time. The fishing was slow, but they didn't seem to care. They were just happy to be out on the boat fishing. Watching Jake outside fishing, you would have thought it was seventy degrees and calm seas. Jake was not dressed nearly warm enough for the cool, wet, fifty-degree day. He had rain pants on, but he neglected to put his rain coat on, and it was just going to be a matter of time when the rain soaked through. It was soon evident that Jake had been using other means to keep warm and "happy." He had been diluting his coffee with something a little stronger and wasn't feeling the elements of the cool day.

MR. FAIR-WEATHER

After a few hours of slow fishing, Doug wasn't feeling much better and had become nervous about the sea conditions. I reassured him the water was fine and we were in no danger from the small waves. With Doug being sick and nervous, and with the fishing being so slow, I decided to make a move closer to town and try our luck trolling for king salmon. The guys had been changing baits and working their rods, but it was evident the halibut were not going to cooperate on this day. Doug went out on deck to reel in his line and let the guys know what the plan was. They soon had their lines in, I had the anchor up, and we were on our way to hopefully catch some kings.

The ride to the next spot was a little rougher than we encountered on the way out. We now were bucking into the waves, and that always made things a little more uncomfortable. But I was still able to keep the boat on step, and we were making good time. The lumpy, bumpy ride was no problem for Jake and Phil, but poor Doug was not a happy camper. He had turned from seasick green to a pale white from fear. I again reassured him the waves were not that big, and we would soon be in calmer waters where we would fish. It was then that Jake piped in with some comforting words of wisdom for Doug. "For Christ sakes, Doug, quit your damn whining. Just think about it like this. It's cold, the wind is blowing, it's rough, and it's friggin' pouring down rain, but who gives a crap? You're fishing in Petersburg, Alaska, and you're having fun." He continued, "It doesn't matter if you're sick or you're scared shitless. You've just got to remember you're in Petersburg, Alaska, fishing, and it doesn't get any better than that." He continued rattling on, "You might get so cold that you can't feel your hands, but that's all right because by God you're fishing and you are having fun. I'll make you a deal. If you go to take a leak off the side of the boat, and your pecker just drops off in the water, then by God you are not having fun anymore and we'll go home. How does that sound?" By the time Jake had finished his fifteen-minute sermon, I was pulling into the new area where we would be trolling for king salmon. To Doug's delight, the weather was much nicer here. The wind was being shielded by an island, and the water was much calmer. I got the trolling motor started, quickly rigged the poles up with fresh herring, and we were fishing again. As we slowly trolled along the massive rock cliffs, Jake gave his expert advice on how to catch a king. He ended his lesson with, "And if it gets off, don't get upset; just remember…you are fishing in Petersburg, Alaska, and you're having fun!"

The first hour of king fishing was slow, but then the day quickly turned. Ted's rod suddenly came to life. His line pulled free of the downrigger, and we were hooked up with the first king of the day. Jake grabbed the rod and handed it to Doug. Doug just held the rod. He didn't have a clue what to do next, even after Jake's presentation of "how to catch a king." Phil and Jake began coaching Doug each step of the way. "Reel, reel, reel…let him run…easy, easy…slowly now…you're doing great." I cleared the other downrigger and lines and just watched the circus. Doug's eyes were ready to pop out of his head with excitement. He had forgotten all about being sick and the rough weather we had encountered earlier in the day. Doug was having the time of his life. Phil and Jake did an excellent job tutoring Doug, and after a nice battle, the king was in the net. It was high fives around the boat as the guys celebrated Mr. Fair-Weather's fifteen-pound king! It wasn't a monster, but it was huge compared to anything Doug had ever caught off a dock. We scrambled to get the lines back in the water, and before I got the last rod down, Jake had a fish on. Jake was a very good fisherman, and within fifteen minutes had his twenty-pound king swimming into the net. We barely got the lines back in the water, and Phil was hooked up with another fish. The bite was on! The day had really turned around, and Doug was now a fishing fanatic. A little nasty, wet weather was not going to be a problem for him anymore. He was hooked on fishing!

With the hot bite slowing down a little, Jake retired to the warmth of the cabin. The rain had soaked through his clothes, and between all the excitement and the firewater he had drunk earlier, he was starting to feel the effects. While Jake tried to warm himself in the cabin, Doug had another nice king on the line. Phil and I cheered him on as he fought the big salmon. He was hooting and hollering as the king jumped out of the water! After a long, hard battle, the big king finally rolled into the net. Doug had landed a thirty-pound king! He yelled at Jake to come and check out his trophy, but Jake remained inside. I went inside to make sure he was okay. Jake was standing next to the heater but was unable to get warm. He was unable to stop shaking. He was cold to the core. This fishing trip was coming to a quick end. We needed to get Jake back to town and in a hot shower before hypothermia set in. I went back out on deck and informed Phil and Doug that Jake was sick and we needed to get back to town so he could get a hot shower. Doug couldn't believe we were quitting. He opened up the cabin door and began to speak, "Jake, what do you mean we have to quit? These salmon are really biting." He pleaded, "You can have the next fish that hits, no matter whose line it's on. We can't stop fishing now. And look, the rain has stopped and the water's flat calm!"

Jake replied, "I'm sick and we need to go in…now!"

Doug remembered how he had suffered earlier in the day, and his response was the perfect touché, "Oh my God, Jake, did your wiener fall off?"

Jake gave Doug an evil eye. "This boat's going to town with or without you, I don't care." he barked.

I started up the boat and headed to town before we had one less person on board. After returning to the harbor, Jake got his hot shower and a hot meal. It didn't take long and he was back to his crazy self and ready to go have a good time. He was in Petersburg, Alaska, and by God, he was going to have some fun.

DROPPING MY LINES

Great Scenery

HAVE YOU EVER imagined what life would be like without the ability to see? I have always taken my sight for granted. No difference between night and day, blue sky, or cloudy days; there is always the same total darkness. I had never really thought about it before. I had the unique pleasure to take John, and his wife, Jan, on a halibut charter. John was in his early sixties and completely blind. This was going to be my first experience of really getting to know a blind person. I will never forget John as long as I live. He really opened my eyes. Also, along on the fishing trip, was another young couple, named Adam and Becky.

Jan and I helped get John aboard. I had him sit on the side of the boat, and then we helped him swivel around on his butt so that he was able to touch his feet on the deck. Jan had me slowly walk John around the boat, up and down each side of the deck, and inside the cabin. I told John where he was on the boat. He touched and felt all around the areas I directed him through. John became familiar with all the pathways and surroundings of the boat. We decided it was a good idea to have him wear a life jacket, just in case he ventured into uncharted territories.

John was excited to catch his first halibut, but he was more interested in checking out the scenery and the different sights. I know, when he told me that, he really took me off guard. John would sit and listen to the different sounds around him and envision what was making the noise and what it looked like. He heard the engines of the boat running, the waves slapping the hull of the boat, an iceberg cracking, and a fragment of ice breaking off and cascading into the water. He would ask, "What is that, and what does it look like?" His wife would paint a picture in words for him. It was incredible. We were all watching the scenery with our eyes, but John was enjoying the scenery and sights far more than anyone on the boat. Have I mentioned that I *love* my job? What a fantastic experience and opportunity for me to get to know this man!

We took our time running to the halibut grounds, stopping frequently so John could enjoy the many sights. It could not have been a nicer day—calm water and a clear blue, seventy-degree August day. It was beautiful.

Once we arrived, I got Adam and Becky set up and fishing. I then got John set up and helped him get acquainted with his fishing pole. He familiarized himself with his pole and reel by feeling it up and down and all over. I put his fingers on the drag and the "let her go lever," and told him these were the two areas of the reel not to mess with. Jan wasn't going to fish; she would just give John a hand if he needed it, which he rarely did. We set John up with a chair on one side of the boat, and Becky and Adam took the other side.

The young couple soon began catching fish. They were experienced fishermen and made my job easy. John was in heaven. He wasn't catching anything, but he heard everyone laughing and enjoying themselves. John had a beer in one hand and his pole threaded between his arms. He heard noises far before anyone else and asked what the sounds were.

His favorite were the humpback whales. He would tell all of us to, "Shut up and listen. Do you hear that? It sounds like something slapping the water." I'd tell him it was a forty-ton humpback whale slapping his fluke on the water. "Magnificent." A few seconds later he'd ask, "What was that? It sounded like a gunshot!" I'd explain to him that it was a breaching whale and that it had completely jumped out of the water. The gunshot sound was the whale landing on the water. He processed what I'd said and smiled from ear to ear.

GREAT SCENERY

John never missed a sound. I had to relieve myself, so I walked up to the bow and let her go. I heard John chuckling from the back of the boat. "Dan, I think I know what that sound is. Are you doing what I think you're doing?" I'm sure he listened and processed a nice picture! Couldn't even sneak a tinkle by this guy. John was good.

John was having a great time. This day was an Alaskan dream come true, even if he wasn't catching any fish. After about three hours of fishing, John felt something shaking his rod. "I think I may have something," he said. He began winding in his fish just like I'd explained to him. Show John something one time and he's got it. He remembers everything the very first time. He was amazing. I can't even remember where I parked the car or where I put my damn sunglasses that are on my head!

It didn't take long and up came a little ping-pong paddle sized halibut. I told John we would let the little guy go "so he can grow up to be a big butt." He was all for letting the small fish go, but first he just had to touch the fish. I brought the lively little halibut aboard and let it settle down from its initial flopping about. Then John put his hands on both sides of the halibut and felt the slimy little guy from head to tail. Now he knew what a halibut looked like.

John caught another little one, but he still hadn't caught one I would let him keep. Becky and John were having a great day too. They had kept a couple nice fish and released plenty of smaller ones. I informed everyone that I divided the fish up at the end of the day. Each fisherman gets an equal share of the total catch, regardless of what they caught individually. It's my boat rule, and it guarantees everyone gets to take home some great-eating fish. The young couple really didn't buy into my program. They had caught all the fish, but they hesitantly said, "Okay, if that's your rule." John insisted that it was no problem if they took all the fish. I told them we would just see what we ended up with, and figure out the split when the trip was over. I left it at that.

At the end of the day, Becky hooked a nice halibut. Everyone was looking down into the water, anxiously waiting for Becky's big fish to show itself. Everyone except John. John was just patiently holding his limp rod and listening to all the excitement on the other side of the boat. Soon Becky's fish came into view, and I bonked him a couple times with the bat and gaffed him aboard.

In all the excitement, we had almost forgotten about John on the other side of the boat. But not for long. I heard him say, "A little...*help!*" We all turned our attention from Becky's halibut to what was going on, on the other side of the boat. A barn door-sized halibut had grabbed John's bait and was taking him for a ride. The fish had drug the blind man, still in his chair, down the side of the boat all the way to the stern. The only place left to go was in the water! I'd told John at the beginning of the day, the absolute cardinal rule is: "Never, ever let go of your rod." I ran over to help him. I loosened the drag, as it was a bit tight. With that tight drag, John was playing tug-of-war with the fish, and in another thirty seconds I would have lost the rod and reel, and possibly a blind man, off the back of the boat!

We got John relocated to where he could fight his fish. John sat in the chair and had the butt of his rod dug deep between his legs, one hand on the rod grip, while the other was cranking on the reel. He was cranking, but the line was going the opposite direction. I would instruct John to quit reeling until the fish was done running, then instruct him to reel until the halibut decided to run again. John had been working on his big fish for forty-five minutes and was getting really physically tired. The fish had worn down, and now it was just a matter of lifting the fish's massive weight off the bottom.

A little help

I had John just lean his pole on the side of the boat and take a five-minute rest. I assured him, "This fish isn't going anywhere. Take a break." Everyone on the boat was concerned about John. This was not in his daily exercise routine. After a little break, John was ready to go back to work. We helped John to his feet so I could put a fighting belt on him. With the butt of the rod pinched between his legs, he was getting a bit sore in the crotch area. The boys were not happy. Using his legs, arms, back, and the support of the belt, John began to move the beast upward. I instructed him to lift up slowly and reel as he dropped his rod to waist level, and to hold his thumb over the line on the reel, so the sheer weight of the fish wouldn't take the line back out. A gain of a few feet on every lift, and the big girl was slowly coming in the right direction. We were in 250 feet of water, and John only had 240 feet to go!

After twenty minutes of heavy lifting, John was seriously gasping, panting, and sweating. I asked what he thought about Adam giving him a short spell. I was really concerned about his health and didn't want to see a good day go bad. John said he was okay, and if there was any way possible, he wanted to land his fish himself. I asked Jan how she thought John was doing. She knew his health better than anyone, and if she said he was okay, I was on board with John continuing. Jan had a very concerned look on her face but sided with her husband.

I began making John take mandatory breaks every eight or ten lifts of the rod. Jan was pouring water in him and on him in an effort to keep him hydrated and cool. After two hours of battling this giant, John had him within twenty-five feet of the surface. His arms were shaking so much that he could hardly even lift the rod. We were only going to get one chance at having John land this fish. If the fish made one last run when he got to the surface, he would have to turn the rod over to someone else on the boat. John was spent!

I got my shark hook out and attached a couple hundred feet of line to it. I told John that when the fish gets almost to the surface, I was going to sink this big hook into the top part of his mouth. I explained that if he takes off to the bottom before I can beat him over the head with my baseball bat, we've got him on your line and on this big line.

Ten minutes later, and the big behemoth's shadow began to show. It looked like a Volkswagen coming to the surface. Thank God John couldn't see. It would have scared him to death. He knew it was something huge from the *Oh my God*s coming from everyone on the boat. I made sure everyone was clear of the shark hook line and stayed out of the way. John made one last pull, and I bent over and rammed the big hook in the bruiser's snout.

The fish was almost as tired as John. Instead of taking off, she just lay there long enough for me to get a couple perfect whacks right between the eyes with the old trusty size 34 aluminum bat. The bat works just as good as a gun. It's all about placement. I followed the two blows to the head with about fifteen more just for good measure. Then I cut the fish's throat to let it bleed out, put a line through the fish's gills and mouth and tied the bruiser off on the side of the boat.

John had landed his big halibut. The battle had taken over two

GREAT SCENERY

hours. Jan helped John into his chair. The sixty-something-year-old blind man had landed a halibut well over two hundred pounds, all by himself. The boat was alive with excitement. John looked like he had just gone fifteen rounds with Mike Tyson, and he had this delirious-looking smile like he'd taken one too many punches. It was a smile that was priceless, and one that I'll always remember when I think of this very special man.

We let the fish hang on the side of the boat for twenty minutes so she could completely bleed out, and hopefully finish the last of her fighting. It's amazing how long a halibut can thrash around after being slapped upside the head with a metal bat and had its throat cut. There's no doubt a big halibut, dead or alive, can be dangerous. Better to let them flop and thrash in the water than to have them do it in a small area on the boat.

Finally, the fish had gone lifeless in the water, and it was time to bring the monster over the side and in the boat. It took two women and two men to wrestle the big mamma into the boat. John just sat in his chair and smiled as he listened and processed all the grunting and groaning going on as his fish rolled over the side of the boat and crashed onto the deck.

Once on board, John immediately wanted to touch and feel his big halibut. I walked him around it so he could touch the sides, tail, and nose to have an idea of just how massive his fish was. He would have to wait until we got to town before I would let him get up close and personal with the fish. It was more than likely the big butt had a few more flops in her, and John didn't need to be anywhere near the area if she did.

On the way back to town, it was a very lively cabin. Adam, Becky, and Jan were reliving the day and John's battle with the big fish. John sat back listening and smiling. Finally, the man with few words spoke, "Ya know," he said, "I was just thinking. You guys weren't too keen on Dan's equal dividing of the catch system. How about if you guys take all your little fish, and I'll just take my one big fish. Or do we like Dan's rule better now?" John was smiling from ear to ear as he said this.

Becky and Adam laughed and both agreed that Dan's fair dividing system was a great plan. I'd completely forgotten about the fish-splitting conversation from earlier in the day, but not John. He remembered everything.

Once we got to the dock, we got the big fish out of the boat. Soon John was actually lying on top of the fish, feeling his halibut up and down and all over. I wish I had a picture to show, but I don't. Just close your eyes and imagine a blind man lying on top and beside a monster-sized halibut…a halibut bigger than him. Now process the image in your mind. John does this every single day of his life! He had taught me that just because you can't see, it doesn't mean you can't enjoy. What a truly amazing man. It was an absolute honor to spend an unforgettable day with him. John's fish weighed in at 276 pounds.

Llama, Llama

IT'S ALWAYS FUN having kids and parents on fishing trips. Let me rephrase that; it's *almost* always fun having kids and parents on a fishing trip. Today was the rare occasion when the parent should have been the one taking the time-outs. It was a beautiful and rare seventy-degree day in July. I had good friends Sue and Craig on the boat, along with George and his twelve-year-old son, Matt. Matt had never been on a real fishing trip before, and he was so excited to go after his first halibut. Matt was a quiet boy, but Sue and Craig soon had him talking and laughing. George, on the other hand, was a talker and not much of a listener. I'm sure this had something to do with Matt being so quiet. George loved to talk about himself and what he did for a living. I would bet that by the end of the day, he would probably have no idea where Craig and Sue were from, what they did, or even both of their names.

Sue hooked the first fish and handed her pole to Matt. Matt was ecstatic. He'd never caught anything over half a pound. Sue, Craig, and George were all cheering Matt on. Matt was all smiles until suddenly the rod went limp. The fish had come off. Poor Matt was devastated. He was doing all he could to hold back the tears. Dad wasn't helping the situation out. George began reprimanding Matt for not keeping steady pressure on the fish and being too jerky with the rod. "You just can't do that and expect the fish to stay hooked," he yelped. As if Matt didn't feel bad enough already, now his dad was scolding him! I reassured Matt and his father that there would be plenty of opportunities to catch another halibut. Matt was not going home without his first halibut. The boat got really quiet for a little while after George's little tantrum.

It wasn't long before George started yakking about himself again. Craig had made the big mistake of asking him what he did for a living. It turned out that George was a farmer. And not just any kind of farmer. He was a llama farmer. I really didn't know anything about llamas, but there was no doubt everyone on the boat would be well educated on llamas by the end of the day!

Thank God, a fish hit George's rod so he could get off his llama speech. We were all hoping Mr. Father-of-the-Year might let Matt have another shot, but then on the other hand, if the fish got off, I might have to put George in a time-out. I think there were at least three people on the boat who were hoping George's fish would get off. I know there was one for positive. Within ten minutes, George had landed a nice thirty-pound halibut. It was a nice fish to start the day. Dad then proceeded to give Son a little pep talk on how not to lose a fish. I didn't have the heart to tell George that it didn't take a rocket scientist to catch a stupid halibut.

Craig hooked into the next fish, and without hesitation put Matt on the rod. Matt grabbed the rod timidly. He was very nervous after what had happened with his first fish. "No worries Matt, if he gets off he gets off. There are lots more of them out there. You're doing great," I reassured him.

While Craig and Sue were laughing and kidding with Matt, trying to loosen him up, Dad was all business, giving orders. "Keep it tight," he said. "No, don't do that. You're going to lose him. Easy no, no." You would have thought he was Matt's drill sergeant.

Matt continued to crank on the rod, nervously smiling while he peered into the water anticipating his fish coming into view. Ten minutes later, Matt's halibut came to the surface, it was a nice forty-pound fish! In Matt's eyes, it looked more like a two hundred pounder. I grabbed my aluminum bat and smacked the fish between the eyes, and in the boat he came. Matt was all smiles, all twelve-year-old boy! High fives from all—nothing better than watching a young boy get his first fish. Dad was happy too.

The day continued to get better. Everyone was getting steady action. Matt was catching and releasing halibut just to keep fishing. This kid was having an absolute ball! George, Sue, and Craig ended up catching their limits, and it was time to call it a day, a great day.

Within the first ten minutes of the trip home, Matt fell asleep. George picked back up on his six-hour-long seminar on the magnificent llama, the most wonderful animal on earth. We listened almost all the way to town about this good-for-nothing animal. We learned how many bowel movements a day an average llama has. I never knew that the llama is a single stool animal. Good information. Craig couldn't take it anymore and decided to rattle George's chain a little, just to test the waters. He said, "So George, isn't a llama basically just a great, big fluffy rabbit? I mean what are they really good for anyway?"

Oh boy, George looked like a rooster all ruffled up getting ready for battle. Craig had him all flustered. He explained to Craig that they were valuable, loyal, and smart animals. Craig couldn't stand it; he had to take one more jab. "Well, I guess I just don't get it. You don't eat them, and they can't pack anything; I guess I'd rather have a donkey!"

George quickly snapped, "They pack things, but just not very much weight at a time!"

Thank God, I was pulling the boat into the stall. No more llama talk. It was time to figure out what everyone wanted done with their catch. George informed me that he had called one of the local fish processors to handle his fish, but he didn't remember which outfit he had talked to. I asked him if it was Coastal Cold Storage, and he thought that sounded familiar. George asked me if I could fillet the fish out and put it in some garbage bags so he could walk them up to the packing plant. Craig and Sue were going to take care of their own packaging, so I just filleted all of the fish and divided the catch up equally.

Craig, Sue, and I gave Matt a hug, George a handshake, and up the dock they went packing three big bags of halibut. They were headed to Coastal Cold Storage with their catch. Little did I know, they were headed to the wrong packing plant! George had actually made arrangements with Tonka Seafoods to pack and freeze his fish, which was the opposite direction.

I quickly cleaned the boat so I could give Craig and Sue a ride home. They both agreed that George had issues…parenting issues and major, major llama issues! Along the way home I was almost to Tonka Seafoods when I saw a young boy with a garbage sack slung over his shoulder, and about twenty-five yards ahead, there was George with a bag over each shoulder. *Oh shit*, they had walked three blocks to Coastal Cold Storage just to find out that they had really made arrangements with Tonka Seafoods, just a short block from the boat. I had sent them to the wrong outfit by mistake. George was struggling in the seventy-degree heat. He was laboring with each step, with the heavy bags of fish hanging over each shoulder. I knew he was mumbling some choice words for me.

I drove by George in the truck, hoping he wouldn't notice us as we passed by. The next thing I know, Craig rolls down his window and says, "Hey partner, I bet you wish you had a llama about now!"

George yelled something about me sending him to the wrong outfit. Hell, I didn't know he had actually made arrangements with Tonka Seafoods. I kept driving. Craig then said, "Sorry, but you've got to admit that guy is a real llama fuck!" I couldn't help it. I started giggling until I was crying. We were all crying, and now whenever Craig calls me up, he says, "Hi, Dan, this is Llama Llama."

Ralph

THIS BOOK WOULD not be complete if I didn't have a story or two about my good buddy, Ralph Johnson, a real one of a kind. I met Ralph one morning about twenty years ago. I arrived at my boat at about 5:00 a.m. to get ready for a 6:00 a.m. charter. I was fiddle-farting around, getting rods and flashers out of the cabin onto the deck. I was in my own little world. Out of the silence came a voice, "Eh?" I looked up and there stood an elderly fellow watching me get set up for the day. My first thought was that he was part of my charter group, and he had just arrived early. Ralph introduced himself and asked if I had room for a straggler to go halibut fishing. I really wanted to take him but had to tell him the boat was already booked by another party for the next four days. "Okay, maybe next time." The gentleman slowly walked away.

The next morning while going through my regular routine getting the boat prepared for the day, I heard a familiar voice. "Eh?" I turned around, and there was the same man I'd briefly met the previous morning. "So, Dan, do you have room on your boat today? I've just got to catch one of those big halibut," he asked. Ralph was very persistent, but again I had to tell the poor guy I was full. He looked at me like he might cry, and down the dock Ralph walked, head down, looking like a lost puppy. Now I really felt bad, but my hands were tied. The boat was booked.

I mentioned my encounters with Ralph to the group I was chartering that day. They were all in agreement that if Ralph was wandering

RALPH

around my boat the next morning, he would be more than welcome to join the group.

When I walked down the dock to the boat the next morning, I could see Ralph wandering around just a few boat stalls down from my boat. I quickly prepared my boat for the day. Ralph soon came walking around the corner and arrived at the boat. Before Ralph could say "Eh," I asked him if he was free for the day to go halibut fishing. He was all smiles. "Really, halibut, today, eh?" Ralph stepped onto the boat. Persistence had paid off. He was like the six-year-old with Mom at the grocery store. If you just keep asking, you will finally get your candy. Ralph was going fishing.

I untied the lines and motored over to another dock to pick up the rest of the group. Joining Ralph this morning was the Smith family, Jan, Randy, and their daughter, Nichole. Nichole and my daughter, Julie Kay, went to college together at Linfield and became good friends. When my wife, Cheryl, and I attended Nichole and Julie's graduation, we became great friends with Jan and Randy. It wasn't long, and the Smith family traveled north to Alaska to see if Captain Dan had been feeding them a line of bullshit about how good the fishing was!

I pulled up to the dock, and the Smith party boarded the boat. Ralph and the Smiths became instant friends. Randy and Jan didn't realize it, but they had just adopted the son they had always dreamed of…Ralph!

Before heading out to try our luck at halibut fishing, Ralph requested a life jacket to wear. The "youngster" was deathly afraid of the water. Randy helped him slip into his preserver, and we were on our way to catch the stupidest fish in the sea! The ride out was full of laughter and a little crying. Ralph was a real tenderheart. (I mean that in a very good way). We soon learned Ralph was from Green Bay and that Brett Favre was God. I should have known Ralph was from Green Bay, as he had on a Green Bay hat, a Green Bay sweatshirt, and a Green Bay coat. He was the ultimate die-hard Green Bay Packer fan. The boat ride to the halibut grounds seemed extremely short with the live entertainment onboard.

I soon had the boat anchored on the spot, and we were halibut fishing. It began as a very slow day, but no one seemed to mind. They were all just enjoying each other's company and new friendships. Randy and Ralph just loved poking fun at each other. After a couple of hours without even a bite, Ralph asked me if I thought there was a chance in hell that we would catch a halibut today. I assured him the dummies would be along pretty soon to snack on our yummy morsels on the bottom. I told Ralph to just have a little PMA (positive mental attitude) and he would soon catch his halibut. Ralph had no clue what the hell a PMA was, but whatever it was he was going to keep it or have it. Whatever he needed to do, he was going to do it until he caught his halibut. Randy took off Ralph's Green Bay hat and exchanged it with his New York Yankees hat. "You have a fighting chance now that you have a real team's hat on." I don't think it was the damn Yankee hat, but Ralph began getting a bite.

"Hey, hey, hey, you guys, look, look, look at my pole!" Ralph's pole took a big bend, and he was hooked up with a nice halibut. He just held on to the pole and watched the end of his rod jerk back and forth. The halibut soon got tired of tossing Ralph's twenty-ounce lead around and surrendered. Ralph brought his thirty-pound halibut to the surface. A couple of bonks to the head, and in the boat he came. Ralph was all grins.

"Okay," Randy said, "now let's catch three more of these damn catfish and go fishing for some real fish." Like me, Randy was a true die-hard salmon fisherman. Halibut are great to eat, but there is nothing like the excitement of a big king salmon on the end of your rod. Jan preferred the halibut fishing but had a lot more patience for salmon since she caught her fifty-pound king on a previous trip. (Someday your fish will come, Randy). I put a new bait on for Ralph, and back to the bottom he went. With a very serious look, Ralph spoke. "You know, guys, if you would do a little less bullshitting and a lot more fishing, maybe you could catch a halibut and we could go salmon fishing. Do I have to do all the work around here? A little help would be appreciated." With some coaching from Ralph, his new family soon caught their halibut, and we were off to try our luck at catching a big fat king salmon…a real fish.

Ralph and his halibut.

While underway, I noticed the chatter level had gone down. When I turned around to check on Ralph, there was just a life jacket where he had been sitting. Ralph only took his life jacket off on the boat for one thing. *Oh God no!* I thought. *Please don't tell me he's in the bathroom making a surprise.* From the crapper, we could hear, "Hey, guys, I think we have a problem." (We? Why is it when someone has a problem it's always everyone's problem?) About that time, the Ode of Ralph began finding its way through the cracks and bottom of the door. Oh my God, it really was everyone's problem! It was an ungodly stench, and it quickly took over the cabin.

Randy knocked on the door. "Good God, Ralph, did you kill a skunk in there?"

The poor souls in the cabin were laughing and gagging at the same time, trying to take in as little Ode of Ralph as possible. Yes, sir, the shitter was full, and the toilet doesn't flush when traveling at 40 mph. It was my fault for not giving Ralph the memo on the rules of the bathroom, but even though it was my mistake, there was no way in hell I was going to offer my assistance. I have a very weak stomach when it comes to raunchy smells, and this totally qualified for raunchy with a capital R. All windows were open all the way. I squeezed as much of my body outside my window as was possible while still steering.

Thank God we had arrived at the area we would be trolling for kings. It was like a four-alarm fire. Everyone and everything evacuated the cabin, being careful not to fall and be trampled by a follower en route to the fresh air on the deck. I began baiting the salmon rods while Randy checked on his new adopted son. "Ralph, are you alive in there?"

Ralph asked, "Hey, what's the secret to making this mess disappear?"

Randy showed Ralph the "Make This Mess Disappear" button, Ralph gave it a few pushes, and all was well again. Ralph had accomplished his mission. (I should have titled this story, "Explosion on the F/V *Julie Kay*.") Ralph came out, Randy helped him put his life preserver back on, and he made his way to the deck to join his now even closer friends. "Hey guys, did I miss anything on the ride over here?" We all just smiled.

We were trolling an area called Blind Slough, Randy's favorite spot. It was a narrow channel that the kings travel to get to their spawning grounds. If the timing is right, this spot can be action packed. This afternoon, our timing was perfect. The kings were here, and they were hungry! I barely got the lines in the water when Nichole had the first king on. While Nichole was fighting her salmon, Ralph slipped into the cabin to get his video camera. By the time he figured out how to get his camera turned on, Nichole's king was in the net. Before I could get Nichole rebaited, Jan's pole came to life. Before Jan could get the rod out of the holder, Randy's rod slapped the water. We had a double. I cleared the other poles out of the way and began directing traffic so the two lines would not cross and break off. Not only was I directing Jan and Randy from one side of the boat to the other, I was also directing Mr. Cameraman in the big, bulky life jacket to move out of the way; Ralph was getting everything on video.

After a ten-minute battle, Jan brought her fish alongside the boat, and I bumped the cameraman out of the way so I could net Jan's beautiful king. Randy's salmon was definitely a much bigger fish. Every time he gained a little, the king would take everything he'd gained right back. Randy was reeling like a man possessed. In the past, Randy has lost a king or two due to the dreaded seals in this area. He wanted this fish in the boat now. After a long fight with the salmon, it looked like Randy finally had the upper hand. Randy's eyes were bulging, his mouth was drooling, and he already had this fat king smoking in his smokehouse back home! Finally, the big salmon came swimming down the side of the boat. With the cameraman by my side and in front of me, I maneuvered the net to get a swipe at the beautiful salmon. The king was now in full view and came swimming down the side of the boat. Just as I went to scoop it into the net, a big furry seal came out of nowhere, and Randy's smoked fish headed for the shore in the seal's mouth! Ralph had the camera rolling and got the whole production, bad language and all, on video. (He has copies for sale.) I put the boat in gear and began chasing after the seal with Randy's fish. The cameraman was still rolling and yelling, "Hey, hey, you guys. Did you see that thing grab Randy's fish?" Every time I got the boat almost beside the seal, he would let go of the salmon. But before Randy could get the fish close enough to the net, the damn furry bastard would grab hold and take off again. I followed the seal almost to the shore. Now the seal only had one way to go, and that was right under the boat, and under the boat he went. When he ran under the boat, Randy had no choice but to lay the rod on the side of the boat when the seal passed by. The outcome was not pretty—more choice words on Ralph's R-rated movie! The rod snapped in two and the line broke. Seal 1, Randy 0. The seal would have salmon for dinner and Randy would have to listen to Ralph. Randy felt terrible holding his half of a pole, but there really wasn't anything different he could have done.

Ralph tried to cheer him up. "Hey, Randy, you just broke Dan's favorite salmon pole in half. Eh, wasn't that a show guys?"

RALPH

I put the half rod in the rod rack and got the other rods back in the water. The next fish that hit was going to be Ralph's. It didn't take five minutes and our cameraman was fighting his first king salmon. I let Randy give Ralph instructions. I just sat back and enjoyed the show. "Reel, reel, reel, Ralph. Don't give that damn seal a chance at another meal." Randy pushed Ralph around the deck to make sure his line stayed clear of the engines. Randy was also giving me instructions, "Dan, get that net ready. This fish is coming in now. We ain't waiting for Mr. Seal this time!" Ralph did as Randy said, and into the net the fish came. Ralph had landed his first king. It would be the last salmon of the day. It was a perfect way to end a charter.

Jan with lunker

Ralph with a real fish

See You Next Year

SINCE THAT FIRST charter, Ralph has been a regular every year, and he always returns with his close friends, Jan and Randy. The Smiths coordinate all of Ralph's travel and lodging plans and make sure he gets from Green Bay to Petersburg and back safely. While in Petersburg, they all stay at the same bed and breakfast, the Nordic House. I highly recommend this place, as Cherise spoils them rotten with all of her home-cooked pastries. Ralph is now in his mid-80s. He has lost a step or two, but is still good ole Ralph, fishing and enjoying life to its fullest. He has become friends with many locals in Petersburg, especially all the good-looking girls. Ralph has quite the trap line. As Ralph puts it: "There's just too many good-looking girls and not enough Ralph to take care of them all. What's a man to do?" (Cindy is his favorite.)

Before Ralph traveled home last summer, I made a date with him to go have coffee in the morning at Pacific Wing. Pacific Wing is a small air carrier, and Ralph wanted to see Sarah, the dispatcher for the company before he left. (Too many girls, not enough Ralph). I stopped by The Nordic House to pick up Ralph. When I went inside, Ralph was watching one of his old DVDs of the Green Bay Packers winning the Super Bowl. In Ralph's world, the Packers never lose.

We drove to Pac Wing, and Ralph charmed Sarah and Cole (pilot) with a few entertaining Ralph stories while we drank our coffee. Ralph received his goodbye hugs, and it was time for teary-eyed Ralph to finish packing for his trip home. On the way back to the B and B, Ralph had a request for me. He wanted to get a rock off the beach for his collection. Ralph gets a rock—a piece of Petersburg—every year, to add to his collection. I drove down to the beach and we began looking for the perfect, special rock for Ralph's Petersburg rock collection. One year, Ralph chose a rock that was shaped like a grenade and was unable to get it through security in his carry-on. Randy was able to get Ralph's treasure later and put in his luggage; it found its way into Ralph's collection. We looked around and finally Ralph settled on his rock. It was a small, shapely little rock that would find a new home in his collection. As we slowly made our way up the beach, Ralph asked me if I could take a picture of him sitting on a log. It wasn't just any log. This log was shaped just like a dinosaur. It looked like Dino on the Flintstones. I took Ralph's camera and got a great picture of him straddling the dinosaur log. Ralph then kind of slid off the side of the log. "Hey, Dan, I think I need a little help." I helped Ralph up off the beach, and we worked our way to the car. We drove back to Ralph's B and B and said our goodbyes. Mr. Tenderheart looked at me and said, "Dan, if I'm lucky enough to make it back next year, am I welcome on your boat?"

I told Ralph the same thing I tell him every year. "The boat will never be the same if you are not on it." I gave Ralph a big hug and walked away before Ralph's emotions kicked in and the waterworks began. Ralph is truly one of a kind.

Ralph on Dino

Epilogue

SEPTEMBER SIGNALS THE end of the charter season. Great blue herons are roosting in the surrounding trees, and the temperatures are dropping. Fog, wind, and shorter days are all telltale signs that another charter season has passed. It's time to unload the boat of all the extra sport fishing gear and just leave the necessities onboard for the upcoming October winter troll fishery.

Cheryl's honey-do list has grown so long I think I'll tear it up and have her start a realistic one. Thanksgiving and Christmas will be upon us before we know it; a time for our kids and grandkids to all get together to celebrate the holidays. Scott (The Destroyer) and his wife, Erica, have two children: son, Gavin, (five) and daughter, Olivia Dawn, (two). They live in Petersburg. Julie (The Informer) and her husband, Eldon, have one son, Grady Wade (two). They live in Juneau, Alaska. There's nothing like spoiling the grandkids and then turning them back over to Mom and Dad. The off-season means Dan gets to settle in and watch NFL football. Between football and holidays, I'll be smoking salmon for everyone to enjoy. Hopefully, if there is enough money in the kitty, Cheryl and I will take a short vacation, maybe to Hawaii or someplace warm. One thing is for sure; I will find plenty of time for winter king salmon trolling. And who knows, maybe I'll start writing another book!

EPILOGUE

Herons

Grandkids Gavin, Olivia, and Grady

Acknowledgements

TO MY WIFE Cheryl for being such a great sport and putting up with me day after day. (My best catch ever!). Daughter Julie for helping edit and having patience with me. Son Scott for helping his dad with all the pictures and computer issues. A big thanks to Klas Stolpe for giving me some great ideas and pushing me not to quit. My brother Dennis for letting me crew on his boats. Troy Curtis for letting me show off your cheek. David Ford for all the great cartoons, you really brought the stories to life. Mandy Kivisto for a spectacular cover photo. Thanks to all of my clients/friends that have fished on the F/V Julie Kay, I would not have a book without you and last but not least, all the fishes in the sea, big ones, little ones, smart ones, and the dummies, please keep on biting!